Bless Your Wife

small gestures to nurture your marriage

365 practical daily actions a husband can take to bless his wife—for Christian men with intention, service, and love in mind.

Dr Chuck Carrington

CONNECT BOOKS

This is a nonfiction work. However, certain sections have been lightly fictionalized or dramatized for illustrative purposes. Any resemblance to actual persons, living or deceased, is purely coincidental.

·

CONNECT
BOOKS
USA

PO BOX 903 Wakefield VA. USA 23888
Connectbooks.pub

Dedication

To all the men I've known and counseled over the years—
God bless you—for earnestly trying to bless your wives,
even when you couldn't quite figure out how… until we
found a way together. Thank you for the stories you
shared—full of frustration, missteps, growth, and, by
God's grace, breakthroughs. One way or another, your
voices live in these pages. I pray this collection, born of
decades of listening, will now help countless others find
their way forward..

Contents

Preface

A Return to Ritual: Why Courting Still Matters

In an age where modern dating often centers on self-gratification, superficial compatibility, and rapid consumption of emotional connection, the age-old rituals of courtship—rooted in patience, intentionality, and communal accountability—provided a more stable foundation for long-lasting marriages. Bless Your Wife is not a book about courtship per se, but it represents a return to the spirit of courtship: the act of consistently attending to a woman with intentionality, reverence, and self-discipline—not for conquest, but for communion.

Before there was "dating" there was *courting*—a slower, more deliberate practice where men engaged women not just to win them, but to know them. Courting was less a game and more a rite: a communal and often sacred act observed within shared cultural boundaries, where everyone more or less spoke the same relational language. Your neighbors knew her family. Her family probably knew yours. There was accountability. There were standards. And there was structure—imperfect, yes, but undeniably anchoring.

Contrast this with modern dating: a largely deregulated, hyper-individualistic experience that mimics a consumer economy more than a path to partnership. The focus has shifted—from learning another person within the rhythms of family, faith, and community, to sampling personalities based on convenience, chemistry, and curated profiles. Today's man is groomed to hunt, to perform, to collect, and often, to discard [think *swipe left—swipe right* process]. Marriage, if it even arrives, can feel like a transactional milestone rather than a covenantal transformation.

This book, *Bless Your Wife*, is not a handbook on courting. It is something both smaller and greater. It is a daily call back to the spirit of courtship—not the spectacle of flowers and dinners, but the enduring rituals of attention and service. The rituals of seeing your wife, choosing her anew, and moving toward her not as a possession but as a person to be pursued even after the vows are said.

Courting wasn't about performance; it was about pursuit with purpose. And while much has changed—culture, technology, expectations—what hasn't changed is this: a woman longs to be cherished, not just chosen. And a man becomes more of a man when he trains himself to bless, not just impress.

Bless Your Wife is an invitation. Not into nostalgia, but into intentionality. A reminder that love, when tended to like a sacred ritual, doesn't expire. It deepens.

Welcome back to the slow, sacred work. .

A Guy's Guide to the Stuff That Seems Silly (But Isn't)

I know—you're a guy, and a lot of what you'll read in this book may seem odd, even silly. That's fair. We're not wired like our wives. Most of us don't care whether the bed pillows are fluffed just right, or if the carpet gets vacuumed once a week or three. We're focused on goals, tasks, peace, and progress. We want to get things done, not get interrupted. We want respect, not decorative soaps.

But here's the thing: those pillows, the folded towels for "company," the seasonal throw blanket that has zero functional purpose—they matter to her. Not because they're practical, but because they're *felt*. For our wives, the little details create a sense of beauty, stability, and care. They experience the world emotionally, relationally, and often intuitively—far beyond what we perceive.

And that's the whole point of this book.

As men, we're often clumsy when it comes to nurturing emotional needs. We don't mean to be—we're just not naturally fluent in that language. But we *can* learn. And when we do, something extraordinary happens: the woman we love begins to flourish.

So, I've put together 365 simple, specific, and tangible ways to bless your wife—one for each day of the year. Small things. Quiet things. Things that may seem unnecessary to you but feel monumental to her. These little gestures become treasures she tucks away in her heart, building toward the kind of fulfillment she longs for (and honestly, that you benefit from, too).

Let's be real. You won't do all 365. No man will. Even if you plan to, or want to, you won't. Life is full. Work, kids, stress, good intentions—it all piles up. But here's the challenge: **do as many as you can, as often as you can**. Maybe over a year or two, you'll get through half of them. If you do that, you'll see a radical change in your marriage—I guarantee it.

To make it easier, I've broken the ideas into 30 themes—things like encouragement, emotional connection, support, intimacy, and more. Most themes include 10 practical ideas, with one exception: the final theme, *Everyday Love*, offers 75 suggestions to help you stay consistent in the daily grind. The plan is simple— pick a theme that fits what your wife might need right now, choose two ideas from it, and do them that week. Just two. Small acts, done intentionally, can change everything.

That's how it starts. And what begins as intentional effort quickly becomes a habit. Not a chore. A rhythm. One that blesses her deeply and draws her closer to you with trust, affection, and security.

Think about it: if you do just two small things each week, that's over 100 moments this year where your wife feels uniquely seen and loved—far more than what most marriages ever cultivate.

How could that not change everything?

Words of Affirmation & Encouragement

"Gracious words are like a honeycomb, sweetness to the soul and health to the body." — Proverbs 16:24 (ESV)

Why it matters: Words are not just sounds—they are signals. For many wives, kind, sincere words are like emotional oxygen. While men might show love through actions or provision, women often feel love through words. Speaking life, calling out her strengths, and affirming her heart builds trust, emotional intimacy, and security.

Plain truth: You might think, "She already knows I love her," but hearing it—especially when she's weary or self-critical—can breathe fresh strength into her. When you affirm her character, not just her appearance, she feels truly *seen*. And that's when she softens, flourishes, and returns that love tenfold.

Write her a love letter

Description: Take a quiet moment to write her a heartfelt letter telling her why you love her, what you admire about her, and how she makes your life better. Keep it honest, specific, and handwritten if possible—it feels more intimate.

Example: On a quiet Saturday morning, while she's still asleep upstairs, he brews coffee and sits at the kitchen table with a pen and a blank sheet of paper. The words come slowly at first—then flow: how her laughter brightens rooms, how her strength steadies him, how her presence makes him feel safe. He folds the letter, tucks it in an envelope, and leaves it on her pillow with a sprig of lavender.

Text her a Bible verse and tell her why it reminds you of her

Description: For example, "Proverbs 31:25 – 'She is clothed with strength and dignity; she can laugh at the days to come.' This verse makes me think of how brave and graceful you are."

Example: During a break at work, he scrolls through his Bible app and stops at Proverbs 31:25. He thinks about how she handled their daughter's meltdown that morning—with calm, grace, and a surprising dose of humor. He texts her:

"'She is clothed with strength and dignity; she can laugh at the days to come.' Reminds me of you this morning. You amaze me."

She replies with a heart and a tearful emoji.

Compliment her appearance today

Description: Notice something specific—her outfit, her smile, her hair—and say it directly: "You look absolutely beautiful today."

Example: She walks into the room, slightly frazzled from trying to get out the door. He pauses, genuinely taken aback by the way her hair catches the sunlight and how effortlessly elegant she looks in her favorite sweater. "Wow," he says, smiling. "You look absolutely beautiful today. That color is perfect on you."

Say "thank you" for something specific she did

Description: Instead of a general thank you, be detailed: "Thank you for making dinner tonight. I know you were tired, and I really appreciated it."

Example: After dinner, while loading the dishwasher together, he turns to her and says, "Hey, thanks for grocery shopping today. I know you were exhausted and still made time to cook this amazing meal. It means a lot." She stops, surprised, then smiles and bumps his hip with hers.

Speak a blessing over her before she leaves the house

Description: Say something like, "I pray your day is peaceful, that you feel strong and supported, and that you remember how deeply you are loved."

Example: She's running late for work, balancing coffee, keys, and her phone. Just before she heads out the door, he grabs her hand, meets her eyes, and softly says, "I pray your day is full of peace, strength, and favor. And that you feel how deeply you are loved—all day long." She exhales, hugs him tight, and walks out with lighter steps.

Tell her, "You're doing an amazing job"

Description: Even in ordinary moments, encouragement means everything. "I see how much you're juggling, and you're doing an amazing job."

Example: Later that night, while she's folding laundry and yawning between piles of mismatched socks, he walks over, kisses her forehead, and says, "You're doing an amazing job. I see how much you carry, and you're handling it with so much grace." She blushes, laughs, and says, "Even with the socks?"

Send her a random voice message just saying "I love you"

Description: Keep it simple: "Hey, just wanted to say I love you. That's all. Just thinking of you."

Example: While waiting in the parking lot to pick up their son from practice, he opens his phone and records a 10-second message:

"Just thinking of you, babe. I love you so much. That's it. Carry on being awesome."

He sends it without context. Her reply: a voice message with her giggling, "You're such a sap—and I love it."

Brag about her to someone else (within earshot)

Description: Talk her up when she's nearby: "She's incredible—she just managed a full day of meetings and still came home with a smile."

Example: During a casual get-together with friends, someone brings up how chaotic their week has been. He smiles, gestures toward her, and says, "This woman right here has been running a marathon—work, the kids, everything—and still manages to be the calm in our storm. I honestly don't know how she does it." She looks up from her drink, eyes wide, and just softly says, "Thank you."

Whisper something kind or flirty in her ear

Description: Lean in and say, "You're my favorite person to look at," or "I still get butterflies when I see you."

Example: As they stand in line at the grocery store, he leans in close, lips near her ear, and murmurs, "You are dangerously good-looking. Like, are you even allowed to be in public like this?" She rolls her eyes, laughs, and nudges him—but her face is flushed with joy.

Say "I'm proud of you" about something she's done

Description: Pick something she's accomplished recently and tell her: "I'm so proud of how you handled that situation at work. You were graceful and strong."

Example: Later that night, as she tells him about how she finally spoke up in a tough work meeting, he listens carefully, nodding. When she finishes, he wraps his arms around her and says, "I'm so proud of you. That took guts, and I know it wasn't easy—but you stood your ground." She closes her eyes and leans into his chest, smiling in quiet relief.

Acts of Service

"Through love serve one another." — Galatians 5:13b (ESV)

Why it matters: Service isn't weakness—it's leadership in action. Many women carry invisible loads—mental, emotional, physical. When a husband steps in and serves without being asked, it tells her, "I see your effort. I'm with you." It's not about chores—it's about shared weight and sacrificial love.

Plain truth: Doing the dishes or folding laundry might not feel heroic—but to her, it's holy. It shows her that her well-being is your priority, not your convenience. Acts of service communicate love in a way she can *feel*, not just assume.

Make her coffee or tea before she asks

Description: Have it ready when she wakes up—bonus points if you remember exactly how she likes it.

Example: The sun isn't even up yet, but he's already in the kitchen, carefully spooning just the right amount of honey into her tea mug. He hears the creak of the stairs and greets her with a warm smile and a steaming cup. "No need to ask," he says. "I've got you."

Tidy up the kitchen before she sees it

Description: Surprise her by clearing dishes and wiping counters so she walks into a fresh, clean space.

Example: While she's upstairs getting ready for bed, he surveys the chaos of post-dinner dishes and spills. He rolls up his sleeves and gets to work. Twenty minutes later, she comes down to fill her water bottle and pauses—eyes wide. "Did you clean the whole kitchen?" He just winks.

Fill up her gas tank

Description: Take her car out and top it off without being asked—it's a small gesture that saves her time and stress.

Example: Noticing the gas light on her dashboard, he swings by the station after dropping the kids at school. Later that day, she gets in the car and sees the full tank—and a sticky note on the wheel that says, "Running on full—just like my love for you." She laughs and shakes her head.

Take over her least favorite chore

Description: Whether it's laundry, dishes, or taking out the trash, do it before she gets to it—without pointing it out.

Example: He hears her sigh as she eyes the overflowing trash bin. Before she can move, he swoops in, ties it up, and heads out the door with it. "I've got the garbage tonight," he says casually. She just smiles and sits back down.

Make the bed and fluff her pillow

Description: A made bed is underrated—especially with a little touch like her favorite throw or a lavender sachet on her pillow.

Example: She steps into the bedroom after her shower and notices the smooth sheets and neatly arranged pillows. Her side even has her favorite blanket folded at the foot and a little note tucked into the pillowcase: "Come rest, beautiful." She melts into the moment.

Surprise her by cleaning her car

Description: Vacuum it, wipe down the dashboard, and maybe even leave a mint or note on the seat.

Example: While she's inside grocery shopping, he sneaks off with her keys and does a quick cleanup—dusting the console, shaking out the floor mats, and placing a peppermint and a handwritten "Drive safe" on the dash. When she opens the door, she just laughs and says, "Seriously?"

Organize a drawer or shelf she's mentioned

Description: If she's commented on a cluttered drawer, take the initiative to straighten it up for her.

Example: She had mentioned that the bathroom drawer was driving her crazy. One evening, while she's out running errands, he empties it, tosses the junk, and uses small containers to sort everything. When she opens it the next morning, she just stares for a second before calling out, "You organized my drawer?!"

Offer to run errands for her

Description: Say, "What can I take off your list today?" and knock it out without adding stress.

Example: He sees her to-do list written out on a sticky note and grabs it before she can. "Tell me which of these I can own today," he says, keys in hand. She blinks, surprised, then rattles off a few. He's out the door before she finishes the last item.

19. Wake up early to take care of the kids

Description: Let her sleep in while you handle breakfast, diapers, or school prep—bonus points if the house is still standing afterward.

Example: She wakes up to the sound of cartoon giggles instead of crying. When she comes downstairs, the kids are fed, the dishes are mostly clean, and he greets her with a coffee and a mock bow. "Morning, Queen. I handled the kingdom for a bit."

Let her sleep in and take morning responsibilities

Description: Quiet the house, get the coffee brewing, and make sure she wakes up to peace, not chaos.

Example: He sets his alarm an hour earlier than usual, tiptoes out of bed, and manages to keep the kids relatively quiet with cereal and coloring. When she finally stirs, the coffee is hot, the house is calm, and her face softens the second she realizes what he's done. "You're my hero," she murmurs, still half asleep.

Romantic Gestures

"Let your fountain be blessed, and rejoice in the wife of your youth." — Proverbs 5:18 (ESV)

Why it matters: Romance isn't just for dating—it's fuel for long-haul love. Small romantic gestures rekindle connection and remind her she's cherished, not just coexisting beside you. A woman's heart responds to intentional delight. It's not about the size of the gesture—it's that you thought of her.

Plain truth: Men tend to think practically; women often connect emotionally. Flowers, notes, spontaneous kisses—they don't fix problems, but they fill the love tank. When she feels desired, not just needed, her heart opens and the relationship deepens.

Plan a surprise date

Description: Make reservations or set up a backyard candlelit dinner—don't let her plan a thing, just tell her when to be ready.

Example: She's folding laundry when he walks in with a grin and says, "Wear something cute. I've got plans at 7." A few hours later, they're eating dinner under string lights he hung in the backyard, her favorite takeout on real plates, and music softly playing. "You did *all* this?" she asks. He just raises a glass.

Leave a sticky note love message

Description: Stick a note on the bathroom mirror, in her car, or on her coffee mug: "I love you more than caffeine."

Example: She opens her makeup drawer and sees a bright pink sticky note: *"You are more beautiful to me than ever. —Your biggest fan."* There's another in her car cup holder. By mid-morning, she's found three, and every one makes her pause and smile.

Recreate your first date

Description: Take her to the same restaurant, wear something similar, and reminisce—it'll spark nostalgia and fresh connection.

Example: He tells her they're going out and hands her an old photo of their first date. When she walks into the restaurant, she realizes—it's the same booth, same spot, same goofy smile on his face. "I even wore the same cologne," he jokes. She laughs, remembering exactly why she fell for him.

Bring her flowers for no reason

Description: Just because it's Thursday. No holiday, no occasion—just you thinking of her.

Example: He walks in the door holding a bouquet of tulips—her favorite. She raises an eyebrow. "What's the occasion?" He shrugs. "You exist. That's enough reason." She kisses him before even putting them in water.

Light candles at dinner

Description: Even a frozen pizza feels intentional with some soft lighting and music in the background.

Example: The kids are in bed, the frozen lasagna is done, and he turns off the overhead lights, lighting two candles on the table. "Date night at home," he declares. She laughs but sits down a little straighter. The flicker of light softens everything—especially her heart.

Dance with her in the kitchen

Description: No music required. Pull her close, sway, and forget the dishes for a few minutes.

Example: As the dishwasher hums and leftovers cool, he grabs her hand and spins her gently. "What are you doing?" she laughs. "We're dancing." There's no music but the rhythm of their breath and the creak of the floor. It's better than a ballroom.

Pack a picnic and take her to a park

Description: Simple snacks, a cozy blanket, and a place to lay side-by-side and talk.

Example: She finds him in the kitchen loading a cooler: fruit, cheese, her favorite sparkling water. "We're going out," he says, grabbing a blanket. They end up under an oak tree in the park, shoes off, cloud-watching like teenagers. It's quiet, easy, perfect.

Put on her favorite playlist and slow dance

Description: She'll light up when she hears "your" song—just hold her and enjoy the moment.

Example: He sneaks into the living room, hooks up the speaker, and starts her favorite playlist. When she walks in and hears *your song*, he extends a hand. No words, just a slow dance while dinner burns a little. Totally worth it.

Give her a spontaneous kiss

Description: No lead-up, no reason—just pull her in and kiss her like you mean it.

Example: She's mid-sentence about groceries when he walks over, cups her face, and kisses her—slowly, sweetly. When he pulls away, she blinks and laughs, "What was that for?" He shrugs. "Because I couldn't not."

Plan a future getaway, even if small

Description: Book a weekend Airbnb, or just make a plan and mark it on the calendar. The anticipation is half the joy.

Example: One evening, he hands her a card that reads: *"Pack a bag for two nights. Mountains. Just us."* She looks up, stunned. "Seriously?" He nods. "We leave Friday. I already cleared your calendar with your sister." She stares at him in awe, already halfway packed in her head.

Spiritual Leadership

"Husbands, love your wives, as Christ loved the church and gave himself up for her." — Ephesians 5:25 (ESV)

Why it matters: Spiritual leadership isn't about dominance—it's about laying your life down in love. When a man prays with his wife, brings Scripture into their home, and invites God into their decisions, it provides deep security. It tells her: "We're not doing this alone—God is at the center."

Plain truth: Even if she's strong in her own faith, when *you* take the lead spiritually, it builds trust. You don't need to have all the answers—just the humility to seek God first. It's not about being perfect—it's about being present with God *and* with her.

Pray over her before bed

Description: Gently take her hand and speak words of prayer over her heart, her rest, and her peace. End the day centered in love and faith.

Example: She's curled up under the covers, eyes heavy from the day. He reaches for her hand and quietly says, "Can I pray for you?" As he speaks blessings over her heart, her mind, and her sleep, she exhales deeply—the tension in her shoulders slowly fading.

Ask her for a spiritual goal and support it

Description: Say, "Is there anything spiritually you've been wanting to grow in? I'd love to help however I can."

Example: During a quiet Sunday walk, he asks, "Is there something you've been wanting to grow in with God lately?" She hesitates, then opens up about wanting to memorize Scripture. That evening, he prints a verse for their fridge and says, "Let's do it together."

Start a Bible study together

Description: Pick a short plan—maybe on love or marriage—and commit to going through it together, even if just once a week.

Example: After the kids are in bed, he pulls out two mugs of tea and a printed devotional on marriage. "Thought we could try doing one of these a week," he says. She smiles and moves closer, already flipping to the first page.

Initiate a devotional time

Description: Set aside 10–15 minutes to read and reflect together, showing initiative in growing as spiritual partners.

Example: He sets an alarm 15 minutes earlier and places a devotional book on the table with her coffee. When she comes down, he says, "Want to start the day reading this together?" She sits, surprised—and grateful.

Encourage her in her ministry or calling

Description: Remind her, "God's using you right where you are—and I see Him in your work and your heart."

Example: She tells him about a conversation she had with a friend that left her unsure if she's making a difference. He wraps his arms around her and says, "God's using you in ways you can't even see. You're right where you're called to be." Her eyes water, but she smiles.

Share a worship song together

Description: Send her a song that touched you and say, "This reminded me of us—I thought you'd love it."

Example: While sitting at work, he hears a worship song that moves him. Without hesitating, he sends her the link with a simple message: "This made me think of you—listen when you get a minute." That evening, she presses play and ends up in tears by the second verse.

Write a prayer for her in a journal

Description: Document your prayer for her, then leave it for her to find—something she can revisit on hard days.

Example: He opens a leather-bound notebook and writes, *"God, give her strength when she feels tired, and joy that doesn't depend on circumstance…"* Then he leaves the journal on her nightstand with a sticky note that says, *"Page 14 is for you."*

Pray with her for your children

Description: Pause together to pray over your kids' futures, choices, and protection—it builds unity and legacy.

Example: As the kids sleep upstairs, he takes her hand and says, "Let's pray for them tonight—just for a minute." They stand in the kitchen, whispering prayers over their son's friendships and their daughter's confidence. The moment is quiet, powerful, and deeply bonding.

Talk about a sermon you heard

Description: Ask her what stood out to her and share what moved you; it turns passive listening into spiritual connection.

Example: Driving home from church, he says, "That part about forgiving before you feel like it really hit me. What stood out to you?" She smiles, surprised by the question, and begins to share. The car ride becomes a sacred conversation.

Fast together for a breakthrough

Description: Agree on a shared purpose, pick a day, and fast together—supporting each other spiritually and emotionally.

Example: They sit at the table with their coffees and decide together: no food tomorrow, just prayer. "Let's fast for clarity about that next step," he says. The next day, in place of meals, they send each other texts like *"Praying now. God's got us."*

Intentional Time

"Look carefully then how you walk, not as unwise but as wise, making the best use of the time…" — Ephesians 5:15–16a (ESV)

Why it matters: Time is currency—and women are deeply tuned to how it's spent. When you carve out intentional, undistracted time with her, it communicates priority. It says, "You matter more than work, phones, or passivity." And she hears that loud and clear.

Plain truth: You may feel that being in the same room is enough. But to her, time isn't about proximity—it's about presence. She needs moments when she feels like the center of your attention, not the background of your schedule.

Set a date night on the calendar

Description: Put it in ink—not pencil. Treat it like a non-negotiable commitment.

Example: He pulls out his phone and says, "Pick a night next week—any night. It's ours." Once she does, he opens his calendar and types "Date Night 🖤" with a reminder set for the day before. She grins, knowing it's not just penciled in—it's *locked in.*

Block off time just for her—no phone, no work

Description: Say, "This hour is just for you." Eye contact, full attention, no screens.

Example: He closes his laptop, silences his phone, and says, "I'm all yours for the next hour." They sit on the couch, talk, laugh, and wander down rabbit trails of conversation without interruption. She doesn't even notice the time—but she notices him.

Do a puzzle or game she enjoys

Description: Whether it's Scrabble or a jigsaw, it shows you value time in her world.

Example: He sets up her favorite board game on the table before she even gets home. "Game night?" he asks, holding up the box with a sly grin. She laughs, sits down, and beats him. Twice.

Go on a walk and talk

Description: No agenda. Just stroll, ask open-ended questions, and listen well.

Example: After dinner, he grabs her hand and says, "Let's walk for a bit." They meander around the block, no phones, no plan, just talking about everything and nothing. Somewhere between sidewalk cracks and sunset, something deep reconnects.

Plan a day around her favorite activities

Description: Spa, bookstore, her favorite lunch— whatever fills her soul, do it together.

Example: He hands her a handwritten itinerary labeled *"Her Day"*—coffee at her favorite shop, a trip to the plant nursery, lunch at that quiet café. "You planned all this?" she asks. "Every detail," he says, already holding her coat.

Have a no-screen evening

Description: Power down everything. Play cards, light candles, talk. Rediscover being unplugged.

Example: He holds up the remote like a peace offering. "What if we didn't turn this on tonight?" She raises an eyebrow. An hour later, they're playing cards by candlelight, talking about high school memories and laughing like it's 2002.

Watch a show she loves even if you don't

Description: Your interest in *her* interests means more than the show itself.

Example: He settles in on the couch and says, "You pick tonight." When the theme song to *her* favorite drama starts, he doesn't groan—he leans into it. Halfway through the episode, she glances over and sees him smiling. *Caught.*

Take her to her favorite café

Description: Let her linger over her latte, and just be present with her.

Example: He surprises her Saturday morning with keys in hand and says, "Let's go to your spot." She orders her signature drink, he gets something weird and seasonal, and they spend an hour sipping and people-watching like college students on a lazy afternoon.

Read a chapter of a book aloud together

Description: Take turns reading something light or meaningful—it's surprisingly intimate.

Example: He grabs a book from the shelf, flips to chapter one, and starts reading in a mock British accent. She snorts, tells him to stop—and then insists he keep going. By chapter two, her head is on his shoulder and her laughter has settled into calm.

Cook together with music playing

Description: Let her pick the playlist. Make something messy and laugh through it.

Example: He cues up her favorite playlist and hands her the spatula. They chop, stir, and dance between countertops while singing off-key. The pasta turns out a little overdone, but neither of them cares—they're full on connection.

__Emotional Connection__

"Rejoice with those who rejoice, weep with those who weep." — Romans 12:15 (ESV)

Why it matters: True connection isn't just physical or logistical—it's emotional. When you meet her where she is emotionally, you create intimacy that no gift or task can replace.

Why it resonates with women: Women often long to be emotionally understood, not just heard. When you engage her heart—celebrating her joys and sitting with her in struggles—it builds a safe place where she can fully be herself.

Ask how she's really doing

Description: Look into her eyes and say, "No filter—how are *you*, really?"

Example: As they sit on the couch winding down from the day, he turns to her, gently takes her hand, and asks, "How are you *really* doing?" At first she hesitates, then the emotion spills out—tears, laughter, frustration, relief. He says little, but holds her through every word.

Listen without interrupting

Description: Let her speak her full thought before you respond. Just *be there.*

Example: She's venting about her day—again—and he resists the urge to fix or jump in. He nods, makes eye contact, and stays quiet until she's completely done. "Thank you for just listening," she says softly. He smiles and squeezes her hand.

Reflect back what she says to show understanding

Description: "So what I'm hearing is…" This simple act shows you care and heard her heart.

Example: She's explaining why something bothered her, and instead of defending himself, he says, "So what I'm hearing is it made you feel dismissed when I changed the subject?" Her shoulders relax, and she nods. "Exactly. Thank you for getting it."

Share how you're feeling—be vulnerable

Description: Even if it's hard, say, "I'm feeling anxious/tired/hopeful." Vulnerability builds trust.

Example: Over dinner, he sets down his fork and says, "I've been feeling overwhelmed lately, and I didn't want to admit it." Her eyes widen—not out of surprise, but because she sees him opening up. "Thank you for trusting me with that," she replies.

Apologize without defensiveness

Description: No excuses. Just, "I'm sorry for how I hurt you. I get it now."

Example: After an argument, he quietly walks into the room and sits beside her. "I've been thinking. I'm sorry I hurt you—I see it now. No excuses." She doesn't respond immediately, but the tears in her eyes say everything.

Affirm her feelings even if you don't fully understand

Description: "I may not totally get it, but I hear you—and your feelings matter."

Example: She's crying over something that doesn't seem big to him—but he takes a breath and says, "I may not totally understand why this hit so hard, but I believe you. And I care that you're hurting." She nods slowly, visibly comforted.

Journal your appreciation for her

Description: Write three things daily or weekly and let her read them.

Example: He keeps a small notebook in his nightstand and, every few days, jots down something she did that moved him—her laughter with the kids, how she prayed over dinner, the way she looked in the morning light. One day, he leaves it open for her to find.

Ask what's been heavy on her heart

Description: Open the door: "Is there anything weighing on you I can help carry?"

Example: They're sitting on the porch swing when he turns and says, "What's been weighing on you lately?" She's surprised but grateful—and begins to talk about things she didn't even know she'd bottled up. He listens without flinching.

Tell her one thing you admire about her character

Description: "You're incredibly compassionate, and I see it in how you treat everyone."

Example: As they watch their kids play, he says, "You know what I admire about you? Your kindness. You're compassionate in a way that makes people feel safe." She glances at him, caught off guard—and deeply moved.

Be fully present when she's talking

Description: No multitasking. Eyes up. Mind focused. She knows when you're really there.

Example: She starts talking while he's scrolling through his phone, and then he catches himself. He sets the phone down, turns his body toward her, and says, "Sorry—go ahead. I'm listening." Her expression softens. Now she really opens up.

Personal Attention

"Let each of you look not only to his own interests, but also to the interests of others." — Philippians 2:4 (ESV)

Why it matters: Noticing the little things—her preferences, routines, or mood—shows that you're tuned in and intentional. It says, "I know you, and I care."

Why it resonates with women: She feels loved when you remember small things, because it proves you're paying attention. This isn't about extravagance—it's about thoughtfulness, which makes her feel seen and known.

Buy her favorite snack and leave it in her car

Description: It's not about the snack—it's that you remembered.

Example: She gets in the car to head to work and finds a little paper bag on the passenger seat with a sticky note: "For the world's best driver (and wife)." Inside? Her favorite dark chocolate and a bottle of iced tea. She laughs out loud and texts, "You're ridiculous—in the best way."

Draw her a bath

Description: Light a candle, play soft music, close the door. Guard her peace.

Example: After a long day, she walks into the bathroom to the scent of lavender and the soft sound of piano music. The tub is steaming, a candle flickers, and there's a towel warming on the radiator. He smiles and says, "Go relax—I've got everything else."

Rub her feet or shoulders after a long day

Description: No strings attached—just a way to say, "I see your effort."

Example: She's curled up on the couch, exhausted, when he kneels down and gently lifts one of her feet onto his lap. "Don't talk—just let me take care of you for a minute," he says. She sighs and leans back, melted butter.

Bring her water or tea while she's reading or relaxing

Description: A small act that says, "You deserve to be cared for."

Example: He hears the soft rustle of pages from the next room and walks in with a glass of lemon water. "Thought you could use a refill," he says quietly. She smiles without looking up from her book, the gesture speaking louder than words.

Create a cozy space just for her

Description: Blanket, soft light, a nook. Make her a retreat.

Example: While she's out, he rearranges a corner of the living room—throws a plush blanket over a chair, lights a candle, and places her favorite devotional on a side table. When she walks in, he gestures toward it and says, "This is your spot now."

Ask about her dreams and goals

Description: "What have you been dreaming about lately?" Then actually listen.

Example: Over dinner, he leans in and says, "What's something you've been dreaming of doing?" She blinks, surprised, then begins to talk—hesitantly at first, then with excitement. He nods thoughtfully and says, "Let's make that happen."

Paint her nails or help her with a self-care routine

Description: It's not about skill—it's about closeness and effort.

Example: She jokingly asks, "Wanna paint my toes?" and to her surprise, he nods. He sits cross-legged on the floor, tongue sticking out in concentration as he fumbles through two coats of polish. She's laughing the whole time—and totally in love.

Make a "just for her" playlist

Description: Fill it with songs that remind you of her or moments you've shared.

Example: She opens her phone and sees a playlist titled "Us." Every song sparks a memory—road trips, late nights, first dances, lazy Sundays. She texts him, "You win. Forever."

Offer a foot massage while watching TV

Description: Effortless opportunity to serve and show affection.

Example: They're halfway through a Netflix binge when he wordlessly lifts her feet onto his lap and starts massaging them. "What did I do to deserve this?" she asks. He grins, "You exist."

Warm up her towel in the dryer during her shower

Description: Unexpected comfort = unexpected joy.

Example: She steps out of the steamy bathroom and gasps as he wraps her in a toasty, fresh-from-the-dryer towel. "You didn't," she whispers. "I did," he grins. "Because you're worth a warm towel and more."

Support & Partnership

"Two are better than one, because they have a good reward for their toil." — Ecclesiastes 4:9 (ESV)

Why it matters: Marriage is a team, not a hierarchy. When you step in as a partner—especially during stress—you create shared strength and trust.

Why it resonates with women: She carries a mental load you may never see. When you step into her world and share the weight, she feels secure and truly cared for.

Ask, "How can I make today easier for you?"

Description: Simple and empowering. Then *do* what she says.

Example: As she's packing lunches and answering emails at the counter, he slides beside her and asks, "What's one thing I can do to make today easier?" She thinks for a second and says, "Could you handle dinner tonight?" He kisses her cheek. "Done."

Offer to do bedtime or homework duty solo

Description: Give her a break without asking her to earn it.

Example: As the clock strikes chaos o'clock, he gently says, "I'll do bedtime tonight. You go relax." She eyes him suspiciously, then retreats upstairs with a novel while he reads *The Gruffalo* in dramatic voices, grinning the whole way.

Attend a meeting or appointment with her

Description: Be her plus-one, even when it's not exciting.

Example: She mentions a doctor's appointment she's nervous about. He clears his schedule without hesitation. Sitting beside her in the waiting room, he holds her hand and says, "You're not doing this alone."

Help her prep for a big task or event

Description: Whether it's packing, prepping, or presenting—your support matters.

Example: She's got a presentation coming up, papers scattered across the table. He brings her coffee, offers to help her rehearse, and quietly runs interference with the kids. "You've got this," he says. And she starts to believe it.

Brainstorm with her on something she's planning

Description: Offer input, ideas, and encouragement without taking over.

Example: She's mapping out her ideas for a fundraiser and he pulls up a chair. "What if we added a raffle?" he suggests, scribbling on her notepad. She lights up—not because of the idea, but because he's *in it* with her.

Support her career or side hustle with time or tools

Description: Buy her a tool, book, or even just say, "How can I help?"

Example: She casually mentions a new tool that would help her creative work. Two days later, it arrives on the doorstep with a note: *"Investing in your dreams is my favorite hobby."* Her jaw drops. He just smiles.

Ask what she needs prayer for at work

Description: Not just how work is going—but what burdens her there.

Example: She sighs while talking about work stress. He looks at her and says, "What can I be praying for this week?" She pauses, touched, and opens up about a colleague conflict. He listens, prays, and checks in three days later.

Be her sounding board without trying to fix

Description: Say, "Do you want advice or just a listening ear?"

Example: She starts venting about a situation with a friend, and he asks gently, "Do you want me to help solve it or just hear it?" She exhales. "Just hear it." He nods—and becomes her safe space to unload.

Encourage her to take a break or day off

Description: Sometimes she needs *your* permission to rest.

Example: He watches her juggling five things at once and says, "Call off the rest of your day—go do something for *you*." When she resists, he adds, "No guilt. I'll handle everything here." Her eyes soften. She actually believes him.

Offer to meal prep for the week

Description: Even if it's basic, it shows you're in the trenches with her.

Example: He grabs a marker and starts labeling containers: chili, grilled chicken, breakfast burritos. She peeks into the fridge and says, "Did you… prep the whole week?" He shrugs. "Thought you deserved one less thing to worry about."

Celebrating Her

"Her children rise up and call her blessed; her husband also, and he praises her." — Proverbs 31:28 (ESV)

Why it matters: Celebration builds honor. When you name her value out loud—especially in front of others—it reinforces her worth and lifts her spirit.

Why it resonates with women: She may doubt her impact or feel unseen. When you celebrate her wins or character, she feels treasured—not just tolerated.

Make a list of 10 things you love about her

Description: Write it out and give it to her on an ordinary day—it'll feel extraordinary.

Example: She finds a folded piece of paper on her nightstand labeled *"10 Things I Love About You."* Each one is simple, personal, and true: *"#3: The way you laugh when you're exhausted. #8: Your unwavering loyalty."* She doesn't say anything—just walks over and hugs him tight.

Frame a photo of you two and leave it somewhere sweet

Description: A visual reminder of your bond, placed somewhere unexpected.

Example: She opens her office drawer to grab a pen and sees a small framed photo tucked beside her notepad— it's them from a beach trip years ago, smiling and sunburnt. A sticky note on the back reads: *"Still my favorite view."*

Buy her something she mentioned in passing

Description: That offhand comment? Remember it, and surprise her with it later.

Example: Weeks after she casually mentioned missing her favorite lotion, she finds it sitting on the bathroom counter. "I didn't even remember telling you," she says. "I did," he replies, "because it mattered to you."

Share a social media post honoring her (with permission)

Description: Publicly affirm her with respect and love—something simple but thoughtful.

Example: He posts a photo of her laughing with the caption: *"Married to a woman who carries grace like oxygen. I still can't believe I get to do life with her."* She sees it during lunch and messages him one word: *"Melted."*

Celebrate a small win in her life

Description: Even tiny victories deserve champagne or at least confetti emojis.

Example: She tells him she finally finished a tedious report. When she walks into the kitchen, he hands her a sparkling water with a sticky note that says *"You crushed it."* There's also a confetti emoji drawn in marker. She laughs so hard she snorts.

Create a little "you're amazing" treasure hunt

Description: Leave clues leading to compliments, a gift, or a love note.

Example: She finds a note on her pillow: *"Clue #1: Go where the coffee lives."* In the cabinet is another note, and then another—each with a reason he loves her. The final clue leads to a small wrapped candle and a card that simply reads, *"You. Are. Amazing."*

Bake her favorite dessert

Description: Even if it's boxed brownies—it's the thought (and chocolate) that counts.

Example: She comes home to the smell of warm brownies and a messy kitchen. "They may not be pretty," he says, holding out a plate, "but I followed the directions *mostly*." She takes a bite and declares it the best thing she's eaten all week.

Throw her a mini appreciation night at home

Description: Candles, affirmations, her favorite meal. Celebrate her just because.

Example: He dims the lights, lights candles, and plays a quiet playlist. "Tonight's about you," he says. He reads a few handwritten notes of appreciation aloud while she eats her favorite meal. It's simple—but sacred.

Make her feel seen on an ordinary day

Description: Look her in the eye and say, "I really see all you do."

Example: As she's doing dishes and answering a text at the same time, he wraps his arms around her from behind and says, "You do so much. I see it, even when I don't say it enough." She leans into him, grateful to be seen—not just watched.

Print out compliments she's received.

Description: From texts, friends, family—gather them together and place them in a jar so she can revisit them anytime.

Example: She opens a small jar labeled *"Reminders."* Inside are slips of paper: things her sister texted, words a coworker emailed, praise he's heard from friends. She reads a few, smiles, and says, "This is... unreal." He shrugs. "Just saving the truth for a rainy day."

Rest & Soul Care

"Come to me, all who labor and are heavy laden, and I will give you rest." — Matthew 11:28 (ESV)

Why it matters: Rest is a gift, not a reward. Encouraging her to slow down and recharge shows that you value her soul, not just what she does.

Why it resonates with women: Women often push through exhaustion out of obligation. When you protect her rest, you're telling her she's more than her responsibilities.

Give her uninterrupted alone time

Description: Take over duties and protect her peace like a bouncer outside a spa.

Example: She mentions needing a breather, so he says, "Go take two hours to yourself—I've got everything." While she journals at the park, he fields kid requests, handles lunch, and guards the front door like a sacred boundary. When she returns, her face says it all: peace reclaimed.

Watch the kids while she naps or journals

Description: Silence and time = true love when life is loud.

Example: He sees her rubbing her temples and says, "Why don't you go lie down or write for a bit?" An hour later, she wakes to a quiet house and a freshly drawn picture from the kids that says *"We let Mommy rest today!"* Her smile is half gratitude, half disbelief.

Set up a worship space with candles and music

Description: Create a sacred corner for her soul to breathe.

Example: While she's out, he clears a corner of the bedroom, adds a comfy chair, her Bible, a journal, and a candle. When she walks in, soft worship music is playing and the space practically whispers, *"You're welcome here."*

Encourage her to take a day off from house tasks

Description: And then *don't* let her feel guilty about it.

Example: Saturday morning, she starts reaching for the vacuum, but he gently intercepts. "Not today," he says, handing her a book and coffee. "Your only job today is rest." She hesitates, then melts into the couch.

Draw her a bath and protect her time in it

Description: No interruptions. Just bubbles, music, and you standing guard outside.

Example: He draws a warm bath, adds lavender bubbles, and puts on her favorite instrumental playlist. As she slips in, he says, "I'm keeping the house quiet— take your time." The kids try to knock once. He doesn't let them.

Set up a retreat day just for her

Description: Plan a quiet day where she can reset and rest deeply.

Example: He books her a massage, makes a lunch reservation, and hands her a printed itinerary titled *"Her Soul-Care Day."* She blinks, stunned. "You planned all this?" He grins. "Every moment. Now go be still."

Send her to a coffee shop with a book

Description: Buy her a drink and tell her to take her time.

Example: He puts $10 in her hand and says, "Go to your favorite café—don't rush back." She spends the next two hours slowly sipping chai and reading her novel uninterrupted. When she comes home, her soul feels three pounds lighter.

Buy her a new journal

Description: Add a note inside: "For your thoughts, dreams, and prayers."

Example: She opens a small wrapped gift and finds a beautiful leather-bound journal. Inside the front cover, he's written: *"Fill this with your dreams. I'll be cheering them on."* She runs her fingers over the pages, smiling quietly.

Sign her up for a women's event she'd enjoy

Description: Bonus points if you handle logistics—kids, calendar, everything.

Example: He tells her, "You're going to that women's retreat—you're already registered." When she raises her eyebrows, he adds, "I took care of everything. The kids are covered. You just have to show up and be poured into."

Take the kids out for a few hours so she can rest

Description: She might just nap. That nap will feel like a vacation.

Example: One Saturday morning, he announces, "We're going on an adventure. You stay here." As he drives off with the chaos crew, she stands in the quiet, stunned. She ends up napping for 90 minutes—possibly the most sacred sleep of her year.

Thoughtfulness

"Let all that you do be done in love." — 1 Corinthians 16:14 (ESV)

Why it matters: Thoughtful gestures show she's on your mind. They don't have to be big—just specific and sincere.

Why it resonates with women: To her, it's not about the gesture—it's about the *meaning behind it.* A note, a snack, or an unexpected favor tells her she's cherished in the details.

Leave a note in her purse

Description: Unexpected love in the middle of her day.

Example: She reaches into her bag during a work meeting and pulls out a folded note: *"You've got this. I believe in you—and I can't wait to hear how it went."* Her whole demeanor shifts, even if no one else notices. She knows someone is in her corner.

Save a memory together in a digital journal

Description: Upload photos and thoughts into a shared folder or app.

Example: After a weekend getaway, he uploads photos into their shared Google Drive album and captions them with inside jokes and favorite quotes from the trip. When she sees it, she laughs—and then tears up. "You even remembered the goat incident?"

Notice and compliment something new (hair, outfit, effort)

Description: "Did you do something different today? You look amazing."

Example: She walks into the room with freshly curled hair, not expecting anyone to notice. "Whoa," he says, looking up from his laptop. "You look incredible. Something's different—whatever it is, it's working." She blushes, caught and flattered.

Play her favorite song when she walks in

Description: Let the house speak love through the speaker.

Example: As she walks through the door after a long day, she hears the opening chords of her favorite song playing in the background. He meets her at the kitchen with a smile and says, "Welcome home, superstar." She laughs and dances her way to the fridge.

Leave her favorite treat on her pillow

Description: She'll smile even before her head hits the pillow.

Example: She walks into the bedroom, ready to crash, and finds a tiny wrapped square of dark chocolate resting on her pillow with a sticky note: *"For the sweetest person I know."* The day ends with her smiling into the darkness.

Send her a message mid-day that says "I'm thinking of you"

Description: It takes 10 seconds and means 10 times more.

Example: She's neck-deep in a chaotic workday when her phone buzzes: *"Just thinking about you. You've got this. I love you."* She takes a deep breath, reads it twice, and somehow feels 40% less stressed.

Make a digital photo album of your last vacation

Description: Title it something sweet, like "Us, Unplugged."

Example: He spends an evening gathering vacation pics into a digital slideshow, complete with captions like *"Best fish tacos in human history"* and *"You, glowing in that sunset."* He sends her the link, and they watch it together on the couch, reliving each moment with grins.

Hide a "thank you for being you" note in her coat

Description: Surprise her when the cold hits with a warm message.

Example: She's rushing out the door on a frosty morning and finds a note in her coat pocket: *"Thanks for loving us so well. You're amazing."* As the cold bites, her heart stays warm.

Surprise her with something from her Amazon wish list

Description: You remembered. You paid attention. You won.

Example: She opens a package she didn't order and finds the cozy scarf she bookmarked a month ago. "Wait—how did you…" He shrugs. "I pay attention to the things that make you smile."

Take a selfie with her and post it to your lock screen

Description: Show her you're proud to be seen with her—every time you check your phone.

68

Example: While they're out grabbing coffee, he pulls her in for a quick selfie, then quietly sets it as his phone's lock screen. That night, she sees it glowing from the charger. "You really put *that* one on there?" she says, laughing. "You look amazing," he replies.

Love Through Touch

"Let him kiss me with the kisses of his mouth! For your love is better than wine." — Song of Solomon 1:2 (ESV)

Why it matters: Physical touch builds closeness and reassurance. It's a reminder that you're connected, body and soul.

Why it resonates with women: Non-sexual touch— holding hands, cuddling, hugging—creates emotional safety. It says, "You're safe here," and it softens her entire posture.

Hold her hand while driving

Description: Silent connection over speed limits and red lights.

Example: They're halfway to the grocery store, small talk fading into quiet. Without a word, he reaches over and laces his fingers with hers. She glances sideways and smiles, saying nothing, but her thumb gently rubs his in return.

Hug her for more than 10 seconds

Description: Long enough to calm nervous systems and say "I'm here."

Example: She walks in from a stressful day, and he wraps her in a hug that doesn't let go after three seconds. No words, no patting—just stillness and breath. Her whole body softens as she melts into the safety of his arms.

Stroke her hair while she rests

Description: No words—just soft comfort in your touch.

Example: She's lying with her head in his lap, eyes closed but not asleep. Absentmindedly, he runs his fingers through her hair, gently and rhythmically. She exhales slowly, a peaceful smile tugging at the corners of her mouth.

Cuddle during a movie

Description: Not just side-by-side—intertwined.

72

Example: The lights are off, the movie's rolling, and he pulls her close, tucking her under his arm. Her feet are on his lap, a blanket over both of them. The movie's good—but being wrapped in each other? Better.

Give a lingering kiss when you say goodbye

Description: The kind that says, "I'll miss you until you're back."

Example: She grabs her bag and heads for the door. He stops her, cups her face, and kisses her—not rushed, not routine. She leaves with a flushed face and a full heart.

Place your hand on her back while walking

Description: A subtle gesture that says, "We move together."

Example: As they walk through the grocery store, he places his hand gently at the small of her back—protective, present, familiar. It's not flashy, but she leans slightly toward him, as if guided by gravity and love.

Offer a surprise back rub

Description: No lead-in. No reason. Just love disguised as touch.

Example: She's sitting at the dining table, working late on her laptop, when he silently stands behind her and begins rubbing her shoulders. "You didn't have to," she whispers. "I know," he says. "That's why I did."

Pull her close and just breathe with her

Description: Synchronize for a minute. Let peace settle in.

Example: The kids are finally asleep. He finds her standing in the kitchen and simply wraps his arms around her. They stand there, breathing in sync, heartbeats matching pace—no words, just connection.

Kiss her hand when you're sitting together

Description: Simple. Old-fashioned. Incredibly romantic.

Example: They're at a coffee shop, chatting between sips. Out of nowhere, he lifts her hand, kisses it slowly, and keeps holding it. "What was that for?" she asks, half-blushing. "Just remembering I married royalty," he replies.

Brush your fingers against hers for no reason

Description: A tiny touch that says, "You still thrill me."

Example: They're walking down an aisle at the store, casually chatting. He lets his fingers trail across hers, catching her off guard. She looks up at him, eyebrows raised. "Still got it," he says with a wink.

Spiritual Growth Together

"Iron sharpens iron, and one man sharpens another."
— Proverbs 27:17 (ESV)

Why it matters: Faith isn't just personal—it's shared. Growing in Christ together strengthens your marriage and invites God deeper into your bond.

Why it resonates with women: Most wives long to walk with a spiritually invested husband. When you grow together, she feels spiritually led, not left behind.

Read a Psalm aloud to her

Description: Let the Word wash over both of you through your voice.

Example: She's curled up under a blanket, tea in hand, when he opens his Bible and says, "Let me read you something." His voice is calm as he reads Psalm 91 aloud, slowly and deliberately. She closes her eyes and listens—comforted, grounded, loved.

Pray for her future

Description: Her hopes, dreams, impact. Lift it all to God.

Example: Before bed, he places his hand on her shoulder and prays quietly: "Lord, bless the work of her hands. Go ahead of her, guide her steps, and fill her with confidence." She doesn't say anything—just squeezes his hand in response.

Ask how she's doing spiritually

Description: No assumptions—just sincere curiosity and care.

Example: One evening over dinner, he sets his fork down and asks gently, "How's your heart with God these days?" She's caught off guard at first, then slowly opens up. The conversation stretches deeper than either expected—and she feels safe in it.

Thank God for her in prayer

Description: "Thank you for the gift of her grace, her faith, and her fire."

Example: While praying out loud before bed, he adds, "And thank You for this woman—her patience, her passion, her strength. She is a gift I'll never take for granted." Her eyes stay closed, but her lips curve into a quiet smile.

Bless her before bed with a short prayer

Description: Lay a hand on her and say, "Lord, give her peace tonight."

Example: As she settles into bed, he leans over, places a hand on her back, and whispers, "God, give her deep rest. Calm her thoughts and carry her worries. Let her feel Your peace." She exhales and whispers back, "Amen."

Send her a Scripture that speaks to her season

Description: Attach a short note: "This felt like God's whisper for you."

Example: She's been anxious about a new transition, so he sends her a message at lunch: "Isaiah 43:2 — When you pass through the waters, I will be with you. This verse made me think of you today." She texts back, "That hit right where I needed it."

Attend church with her eagerly

Description: Be engaged. Sing. Serve. Sit close.

Example: Sunday morning, he's up early, shirt ironed, coffee ready for both of them. At church, he wraps an arm around her during worship and joins in without hesitation. She doesn't say it, but it means the world to her.

Begin a short devotional together

Description: Even one-page a day draws your hearts closer.

Example: He picks up a simple 30-day couple's devotional and says, "What if we did this over breakfast for the next month?" They start the next morning—ten minutes, one page, one shared moment of spiritual alignment that sets the tone for the day.

Share your testimony with her again

Description: She may know the story—but not the details that shaped your faith.

Example: One evening, he starts sharing the full story of how he came to faith—the real details, the turning point, the prayer that changed him. She listens closely, hearing parts she'd never known. "Thank you for letting me see that part of your heart," she says afterward.

Tell her how you've seen God grow her

Description: "Your patience this year has been such a reflection of Christ."

Example: As they're driving home one evening, he turns and says, "I've seen so much growth in you—especially how you've handled conflict with grace. God's clearly doing something beautiful in you." Her silence is reverent. Affirmation hits differently when it's spiritual.

Sharing Her Story

"Out of the abundance of the heart the mouth speaks."
— Luke 6:45b (ESV)

Why it matters: When you ask about her past, her memories, and her dreams, you learn how to love her better in the present.

Why it resonates with women: She doesn't want you to just know *her now*—she wants her *whole story* honored. It builds emotional closeness and trust.

Record her telling a meaningful story

Description: Ask her to share a memory or moment that shaped her—record it as a keepsake.

Example: He pulls out his phone and says, "Tell me about the day you got that scholarship again—I want to remember it exactly how you tell it." As she speaks, he hits record. Later, he titles the file *"The Day She Knew She Could Fly."*

Ask her about her childhood dreams

Description: "What did little you want to be? Do any of those dreams still linger?"

Example: One quiet evening, he asks, "When you were ten, what did you want to be when you grew up?" She lights up, talking about writing books and being a vet. He listens, then says, "I still see the storyteller in you."

Help her journal goals or prayers

Description: Sit down with her, pen in hand, and ask what she wants to write down for her future.

Example: He brings her a new notebook and says, "Let's dream out loud. What's on your heart this season?" They sit on the porch and jot down hopes, prayers, and bucket list ideas—his, hers, theirs.

Interview her about her life and write it down

Description: Treat her like the subject of a meaningful biography—because she is.

Example: He sits across from her with a notebook and says, "Tell me about your first best friend. And your favorite teacher." She laughs, then starts talking. He writes down every detail like it's sacred—and it is.

Create a memory scrapbook

Description: Photos, captions, ticket stubs—anything that says, "We've lived this beautiful life."

Example: She opens a scrapbook and flips through pages of moments: concert tickets, goofy Polaroids, notes in his handwriting. Each page whispers, *"I remember. I treasure this. I treasure you."*

Print meaningful photos

Description: Frame them, put them in a book, or pin them somewhere she'll see every day.

Example: He picks up some prints from the pharmacy—her with the kids, their last trip, one where she's laughing mid-sentence. He quietly hangs them along the staircase. She notices days later, stops, and tears up.

Listen to a song she connects with and ask why

Description: "Why does this song speak to you?" Then just sit in her answer.

Example: She plays a melancholy song while folding laundry. He sits beside her and says, "You've played this one a lot lately. What does it mean to you?" Her answer is more than lyrics—it's heart-deep. He listens without interruption.

Read her old blog or social posts and talk about them

Description: Celebrate her voice—whether reflective, passionate, or hilarious.

Example: He scrolls through an old blog post she wrote in college and reads it aloud with a smile. "This line right here—'faith feels like walking barefoot in the dark'—you wrote that?" She blushes. "Yeah." "It's brilliant," he says. "So are you."

Ask her to share her testimony over dinner

Description: Even if you've heard it before, she might tell it differently this time.

Example: Over a candlelit dinner, he says softly, "Will you tell me your testimony again?" She pauses, then begins—and this time, includes new layers of fear, grace, and growth. He listens like it's the first time he's ever heard her speak.

Watch a movie that shaped her childhood

Description: Watch it through her eyes. Let her nostalgia become your connection.

Example: She cues up *The Parent Trap* with excitement, and he settles in next to her, ready to endure the cheese. But as she quotes every line and laughs before the punchlines, he starts to see it: this silly movie shaped little pieces of the woman he loves.

Daily Practical Blessings

"Do not neglect to do good and to share what you have, for such sacrifices are pleasing to God." — Hebrews 13:16 (ESV)

Why it matters: Small, everyday acts—like making lunch or running errands—build a life of service and care.

Why it resonates with women: She feels supported when you handle real-life tasks. It tells her, "You're not in this alone."

Make her lunch for work

Description: Even if it's just a sandwich, it speaks volumes.

Example: She opens her lunch bag and finds a neatly packed container, a folded napkin, and a little sticky note: *"Fuel for the boss lady. I love you."* She laughs, takes a bite, and texts, "You win. Again."

Replace a household item she uses often

Description: Notice the little things she needs before she asks.

Example: He notices her phone charger cord is fraying and orders a new one without telling her. The next morning, it's plugged in beside her nightstand with a note: *"I've got your back—and your battery."*

Sharpen her kitchen knives or clean her tools

Description: Unseen care behind the scenes makes her work easier.

Example: She grabs her favorite knife to chop vegetables and pauses. "Did you sharpen this?" she calls out. "Yep," he replies. "Sharp tools for a sharp woman."

Fix something that's been broken

Description: Even if she stopped asking, take care of it and let her be surprised.

Example: The cabinet door that's been hanging crooked for months suddenly swings perfectly. She notices and calls out, "Wait—did you fix this?" From the other room, he grins, "Maybe. Maybe I'm a ninja."

Wash and vacuum her car

Description: She'll feel appreciated from the moment she opens the door.

Example: She opens her car and smells lemon-clean instead of kid crumbs and old receipts. There's even a little air freshener hanging with the word *"Loved."* She texts him: *"Did you trade my car for a new one?"*

Stock her favorite coffee/tea/snack

Description: When she sees it in the pantry, she'll know: "He knows me."

Example: She reaches for a mug and sees her favorite obscure herbal tea restocked on the shelf. "You remembered?" she asks. He nods. "Of course. You always reach for it when life gets loud."

Update her phone background with a meaningful quote

Description: Find a verse, line, or phrase that speaks life.

Example: She unlocks her phone and pauses. Instead of her usual wallpaper, it's a floral graphic that reads, *"You are deeply loved and wildly capable."* "How did you…?" He shrugs. "Hacked it with love."

Print out a coupon or voucher she can use for you (e.g. 1-hour nap time)

Description: Make it playful, creative, and real. Then honor it.

Example: She finds a handmade "coupon" on the kitchen table: *"Redeem for 1 hour of uninterrupted rest, complete with coffee delivery."* She cashes it in immediately—and he delivers.

Set a reminder for an anniversary or milestone and celebrate it early

Description: Early thoughtfulness wins every time.

Example: Three days before the anniversary of her business launch, he surprises her with flowers and a card: *"You started something brave—and I'll never stop cheering for you."* She didn't even remember the date. He did.

Refill her daily vitamin or meds organizer

Description: It's not just responsible—it's tender.

Example: She opens the pill case expecting to do her usual refill—and finds it already done. Everything's in its place, and there's a Post-it stuck on the lid: *"Because you're worth the little things, too."*

Dates & Togetherness

"Therefore what God has joined together, let not man separate." — Mark 10:9 (ESV)

Why it matters: Intentional time together guards your unity. Dating your wife communicates, "I still choose you."

Why it resonates with women: She doesn't just want your time—she wants your *attention*. Dates keep the relationship from turning into a routine.

Try a brand-new restaurant

Description: Break the routine. Go somewhere neither of you have been.

Example: He pulls up a reservation confirmation on his phone. "It's called 'The Wandering Fork.' No clue what they serve, but I heard good things." She smiles—he's always down to try something new with her.

Do a couple's workout together

Description: Laugh through the awkwardness and cheer each other on.

Example: They're in the living room, following a YouTube workout. She's graceful; he's flailing. But they're both laughing, sweating, and high-fiving through the chaos. "We survived!" he gasps. "Barely," she teases.

Visit a meaningful place from your past

Description: Go back to where you first met or dated. Walk down memory lane—literally.

Example: He drives her to the bench where they had their first long talk years ago. They sit, share old stories, and realize how much has changed—and how much hasn't.

Explore a farmer's market

Description: Stroll, sample, hold hands, and buy something quirky for her.

Example: They wander between booths, sampling jams and giggling at homemade soap names. He buys her a tiny cactus. "It's low-maintenance," he says. "But still cute." She smirks. "Just like you."

Make homemade pizzas together

Description: She chooses toppings. You fight over crust. It's perfect.

Example: The kitchen's a mess, the dough is lopsided, and there's flour in her hair. But the laughter is constant, and the pizza's better than takeout. "We should open a restaurant," he jokes. "We'd go bankrupt," she says, still laughing.

Go for a night walk

Description: The quiet, the dark, and just you two. Soul-deep conversations tend to happen here.

Example: They walk under streetlamps in hoodies and sneakers, talking about fears, plans, and funny kid stories. The world feels quieter at night. So do their hearts. But somehow, more connected.

Book a staycation

Description: You don't have to travel far to get away—just disconnect from normal.

Example: He books a hotel 15 minutes from home. No chores, no schedule, just robes, room service, and each other. "This was better than a road trip," she says. "Fewer blisters," he agrees.

Watch the sunset or sunrise together

Description: Start or end your day in awe—with her.

Example: They drive to a hilltop, sit on the hood of the car, and sip coffee while the sky turns from gold to pink. "We don't do this enough," she whispers. "Let's start doing it more," he replies.

Build a fort or cozy corner for a movie night

Description: Get silly, get creative, and get close under the pillows and blankets.

Example: He surprises her with a fort in the living room—pillows, blankets, fairy lights. "It's structurally questionable," he says. "But 100% cuddle-approved." They spend the night like kids in love.

Take her on a spontaneous day trip

Description: Pack snacks, pick a direction, and go. Adventure = bonding.

Example: He walks in with sunglasses and says, "Grab your shoes—we're leaving in 10. I don't know where we're going, but snacks are packed." They end up in a tiny town, trying weird sodas and laughing at old antique stores. No plan, no pressure. Just them.

Creativity & Fun

"A joyful heart is good medicine." — Proverbs 17:22a (ESV)

Why it matters: Fun keeps your marriage fresh. Creativity brings playfulness and connection that strengthens intimacy.

Why it resonates with women: She wants to laugh with you, not just live beside you. When you make room for joy, you invite her heart to rest.

Do a DIY project together

Description: Build, paint, or assemble something as a team—even if it ends up crooked.

Example: They decide to build a shelf. He reads instructions, she eyeballs things. Halfway through, they're covered in sawdust, debating which way is "up." But the laughter never stops—and the shelf almost holds books.

Paint mugs or pottery at a local studio

Description: Unleash your inner Picasso—even if it ends up in the back of the cupboard.

Example: They sit at a pottery café, each painting a mug. His says "World's Okayest Husband," hers has hearts and flowers. Neither are masterpieces, but both go home full of color, creativity, and closeness.

Build something small for her (a shelf, a photo frame)

Description: Use your hands to make something she'll use with her heart.

Example: He surprises her with a handmade wooden photo frame, slightly uneven but beautiful. Inside, a picture of them from their last trip. She touches it and says, "You made this?" He nods. "Every crooked corner."

Write her a short poem

Description: Sweet, silly, or serious—it doesn't have to rhyme to be romantic.

Example: She finds a note in her journal:

Roses are overrated. You're not.

This is short, because dinner's burning.

But I love you more than tacos.

She laughs out loud and pins it to the fridge.

Take silly photos together

Description: Let go of dignity for the sake of joy.

Example: While out on a walk, he pulls out his phone and says, "Funny face selfie?" They make ridiculous expressions, burst into laughter, and end up with 20 blurry, joyful shots. She saves one as her lock screen.

Learn a TikTok dance or fun reel just for laughs

Description: The more offbeat, the better. Laughing together keeps you young.

Example: They spend an hour in the kitchen trying to mimic a TikTok dance. He's terrible. She's not much better. But when they finally nail 5 seconds of it, they cheer like they won Olympic gold.

Make a playlist of songs that tell your love story

Description: Chronicle your relationship through music—first dates, wedding, road trips.

Example: He creates a playlist titled *"Us in Songs"* and texts her the link. The first song is the one that played on their first date. The last one is the lullaby they sang to their baby. She listens and cries the whole drive home.

Draw or sketch something just for her

Description: Stick figures count. The point is effort, not art.

Example: She finds a doodle on the counter: it's her, him, and a heart between them, drawn in pen on a napkin. "My love is more talented than my drawing," the caption reads. She tapes it to the fridge anyway.

Create a memory jar together

Description: One note per week, one memory per slip. Watch it grow.

Example: He hands her a jar and some small paper squares. "Let's write down our favorite moment each week," he says. She drops the first one in: *"That time you made pancakes at midnight just because I was sad."*

Try something you've never done together

Description: New experiences create new connection.

Example: He signs them up for a beginner's archery class. "We may lose an arrow or two," he jokes. She rolls her eyes, but by the end, they're both laughing, sore, and totally hooked on the idea of being beginners—together.

Unspoken Gestures

"Let us not love in word or talk but in deed and in truth." — 1 John 3:18 (ESV)

Why it matters: Actions—especially the quiet ones—prove your words. Love shown in deeds builds credibility and comfort.

Why it resonates with women: She notices what you think goes unnoticed. Gentle gestures, like warming her car or making coffee, feel like love wrapped in silence.

Smile at her from across the room

Description: That knowing look that says, "Still crazy about you."

Example: At a gathering, she catches him watching her from across the room. He smiles—a slow, warm, unmistakably *her*-focused smile. Her stomach flips like it did when they were first dating.

Warm her side of the bed

Description: Lie there for a minute before she gets in. Winter romance, solved.

Example: She comes out of the bathroom and climbs into bed, instantly cozy. "Did you warm it up for me?" she asks. "Of course," he replies. "I'm basically your electric blanket."

Let her pick the movie

Description: No sighs. No sarcasm. Just popcorn and full attention.

Example: She queues up a rom-com he's definitely seen twice. He smiles, wraps an arm around her, and says, "I'm all in." She doesn't even care if he watches the whole thing—she just loves that he's there.

Offer her your jacket when she's cold

Description: Chivalry lives in small, thoughtful warmth.

Example: She shivers walking to the car, and without a word, he slides his jacket around her shoulders. "But now you'll be cold," she says. "Yeah," he shrugs. "But you'll be warm."

Wait up for her when she's out late

Description: Even if you're tired, show her she's worth the wakefulness.

Example: She comes home from a girls' night and finds him on the couch, half-asleep but still up. "You didn't have to wait," she whispers. "I know," he says, eyes barely open. "But I like seeing you safe."

Let her win (or try to!)

Description: Competitive spirit can take a back seat to joy.

Example: They play Scrabble, and she lays down a questionable word. He raises an eyebrow, then says, "I'll allow it." She knows he knows—but she also knows he's letting love win this round.

Reach for her hand first

Description: Be the initiator of connection.

Example: As they walk through the parking lot, he casually reaches over and grabs her hand. No ceremony, no prompt—just instinct. She smiles and squeezes back.

Tuck her in gently if she falls asleep early

Description: Kiss her forehead, turn off the light, and let her rest.

Example: She's curled up on the couch, dozing with a book on her chest. He covers her with a blanket, kisses her forehead, and whispers, "Sweet dreams, babe." She stirs, but doesn't wake—already safe.

Pick her up from somewhere just because

Description: Surprise her with convenience, care, and presence.

Example: She texts that she's about to Uber home. Ten minutes later, he pulls up in front of the café. "Figured I'd come get my favorite person instead," he says. She climbs in, glowing.

Stand when she walks in the room

Description: Old-school honor never goes out of style.

Example: At a dinner with friends, she returns from the restroom and he subtly rises as she approaches the table. It's brief—but she notices. So does everyone else. That's the point.

Spiritual Encouragement

"Therefore encourage one another and build one another up…" — 1 Thessalonians 5:11 (ESV)

Why it matters: Your words can strengthen her soul. Encouraging her spiritually shows that you care about what matters most.

Why it resonates with women: She may quietly doubt herself. When you speak truth and identity over her, she feels seen not just by you—but by God.

Send her a note with your favorite devotional

Description: Share something that's been feeding you and invite her into it.

Example: He snaps a photo of a paragraph from his morning devo and texts it to her with a message: *"This reminded me of your courage."* Later that night, she says, "That one line stuck with me all day."

Leave her Bible open to a meaningful verse

Description: Mark a Scripture she might need today— and say why.

Example: She finds her Bible open on the table, a sticky note flagging Psalm 34:18: "The Lord is close to the brokenhearted…" His note says, "For when the weight feels like too much. He's near. And so am I."

Post a Scripture on your bathroom mirror

Description: A daily glance that reminds both of you what matters most.

Example: She notices a new index card taped to the mirror: *"Let all that you do be done in love – 1 Corinthians 16:14."* Her mascara hand pauses mid-air as she reads. Her day now starts in truth.

Pray blessings over her side of the bed

Description: While she's not there, whisper prayers into her space.

Example: Before crawling into bed, he lays a hand on her pillow and prays, "God, meet her in her sleep. Heal what's weary. Remind her she's cherished." She'll never know—but heaven hears it.

Start a "prayers for my wife" journal

Description: Write out prayers over time—her legacy in ink.

Example: Tucked in his nightstand is a small notebook. Each page starts with *"Today, I prayed…"* When she stumbles on it by accident, she reads five years' worth of prayers—and cries like it's sacred.

Ask how God has been speaking to her

Description: Not "has He?" but "how?"—assume He's moving.

Example: Over coffee, he says, "What's God been whispering to you lately?" Her face lights up. She shares something small, but meaningful. He nods, soaking in her wisdom like water.

Write out a personalized blessing from Scripture

Description: Insert her name into a verse and give it to her as a declaration.

Example: He slips her a card that reads: *"May [Her Name] be like a tree planted by streams of water… bearing fruit in season."* (Psalm 1) She reads it twice, then tucks it into her Bible forever.

Make a prayer board for your home

Description: List requests, dreams, and names you're lifting up together.

Example: He mounts a small corkboard near the kitchen with sections labeled *"Needs," "Thanks,"* and *"Waiting."* Together, they pin up names and hopes. It becomes more than decoration—it becomes rhythm.

Talk about a character in the Bible you both admire

Description: Faith convos don't always need application—sometimes they just connect.

Example: On a lazy afternoon walk, he says, "I've always admired Ruth's loyalty. Who do you connect with?" She thinks for a moment and says, "Deborah. She was gentle *and* strong." They walk in silence, pondering, smiling.

Celebrate a spiritual milestone (baptism, mission trip, etc.)

Description: Mark it with joy like you would a birthday or promotion.

Example: She casually mentions it's been 10 years since her baptism. That night, he brings home flowers and a card that says, *"Ten years walking with Jesus—and me. You're more radiant than ever."*

Protecting Her Heart

"Above all else, guard your heart, for everything you do flows from it." — Proverbs 4:23 (NIV)

Why it matters: Your role is not just to protect her physically—but emotionally and spiritually. That means being trustworthy and gentle.

Why it resonates with women: She needs to know her heart is safe with you—no sarcasm, betrayal, or carelessness. Safety breeds intimacy.

Guard your time and attention

Description: Your intentional focus is her emotional safety net.

Example: She walks into the room and he closes his laptop without being asked. "You have my eyes," he says. She doesn't say much—but her whole demeanor softens.

Speak positively about her when she's not around

Description: Honor her even when she'll never hear it.

Example: At lunch with a friend, he casually says, "Honestly, I don't know how she does it all—and stays kind." No one else reports it. But he knows what he said—and so does God.

Turn off or step away from distractions when she needs you

Description: Give her more than presence—give her attention.

Example: She starts sharing something heavy, and mid-scroll, he sets his phone face down. "I'm all ears," he says. She keeps talking—because she knows she's being *heard*.

Reassure her of your commitment

Description: Say the quiet things out loud: "I'm not going anywhere."

106

Example: After a hard conversation, he pulls her close and whispers, "I'm still here. I'm *always* here." She doesn't need solutions—just the safety of his resolve.

Tell her why you still choose her

Description: Not just "I love you," but "I love you *because...*"

Example: On an ordinary Tuesday, he turns to her and says, "You're still the most courageous woman I've ever known. That's why I chose you—and I'd choose you again today." She doesn't say much—but she's holding it in her chest all week.

Be honest and gentle in conflict

Description: Speak truth without harshness—build bridges, not walls.

Example: They disagree—heatedly. But instead of withdrawing, he says, "I'm frustrated, but I'm for you. Let's figure this out." The tension lowers. Love rises.

Apologize without excuses

Description: Own your part. No defense. Full humility.

Example: After raising his voice, he later sits down beside her and says, "I was wrong. I'm sorry. No excuses." She exhales and whispers, "Thank you." Peace has room to return.

Ask for forgiveness for something overlooked

Description: Don't wait for her to bring it up—bring it yourself.

Example: "I realized I've been distracted lately and haven't been showing up like I should," he says. "I'm sorry. Will you forgive me?" She blinks, surprised—and says yes before the sentence finishes.

Set boundaries with others to protect your marriage

Description: No gray lines—just clear honor.

Example: He tells a coworker who crosses a line, "I don't talk about my marriage like that—and I'd appreciate it if we kept things professional." No announcement at home, but that quiet moment shields his wife's heart more than she'll ever know.

Avoid sarcasm or jokes at her expense

Description: Your humor should build, never bruise.

Example: Someone cracks a joke at her during a game night. He doesn't laugh. Instead, he says, "Nah, not my wife. She's a legend." She meets his eyes—silent, grateful, deeply safe.

Encouraging Her Dreams

"And let us consider how to stir up one another to love and good works." — Hebrews 10:24 (ESV)

Why it matters: When you believe in her dreams, you build her confidence. It shows your love isn't just about who she is—it's about who she's becoming.

Why it resonates with women: Many women put dreams on hold for others. When you cheer her on, you're saying, "You don't have to shrink to be loved."

Ask about her goals for the next year

Description: Invite her vision forward: "What's something you'd love to grow in or start?"

Example: Over a quiet dinner, he asks, "If you could accomplish one thing this year, what would it be?" She pauses—then lights up. As she talks, he listens like her dreams are the most important thing on the table.

Offer to invest time or money into one of her dreams

Description: Be her sponsor. Her investor. Her biggest bet.

Example: She mentions wanting to take an online design course but feels guilty about the cost. The next morning, she finds a note: *"Enrolled. Paid. Cheering you on."* Her eyes well up. He believed in her—before she even did.

Watch the kids so she can work or create

Description: Protect her space to pursue what makes her soul come alive.

Example: He tells her, "Saturday morning is yours—no interruptions." While she disappears into her writing nook, he handles the chaos with the kids. Later, she emerges with ink-stained hands and joy in her eyes.

Read her blog, art, or writing and give feedback

Description: Don't skim. Read it like it matters—because it does.

Example: She sends him a new blog post and nervously waits. An hour later, he texts: *"That third paragraph? That's gold. You captured something sacred."* She breathes out relief. He saw her.

Set up a workspace for her

Description: A quiet table, a clean desk, a corner that says "You belong here."

Example: She comes home to find her favorite lamp, a new notepad, and a sign that reads *"Create boldly."* "It's your space now," he says. "The world needs what you carry."

Ask about her bucket list

Description: Dream out loud together—and keep dreaming.

Example: One night, he grabs a pen and says, "Let's list ten things you want to do in your lifetime." She laughs, then starts writing. By the end, they have a list, a plan, and renewed excitement for what's ahead.

Share her work with someone you admire

Description: Use your voice to elevate hers.

Example: He forwards her small business Instagram to a friend and says, "She's insanely talented—take a look." When she finds out later, her cheeks flush with pride. She didn't know he was her marketing team too.

Speak vision over her life

Description: Not just what she's done—but what she's *becoming.*

Example: He looks her in the eyes and says, "I see a leader in you. A woman who builds things that last." She doesn't respond right away—because she's still trying to believe he means it. But he does.

Offer to fund a class or course for her

Description: Learning is self-investment—help her take the step.

Example: He surprises her with a gift card and a handwritten list of local classes she'd love: photography, pottery, writing. "Pick one," he says. "Better yet—pick two."

Tell her you believe in her—even when she doesn't

Description: When doubt shows up, be louder with truth.

Example: She confesses she feels like she's not good enough to chase her goals. He pulls her close and says, "You may doubt yourself, but I never have. I believe in what's in you—and I always will."

Everyday Appreciation

"Give thanks in all circumstances…" — 1
Thessalonians 5:18a (ESV)

Why it matters: Gratitude softens hearts and
strengthens connection. Appreciation makes her feel
valued—not taken for granted.

Why it resonates with women: She often works
behind the scenes. Noticing her efforts tells her, "You
matter. I see you."

Thank her for something she did today

Description: Small, specific gratitude builds lasting warmth.

Example: He walks past the made bed and calls out, "Thanks for doing that today—I noticed." She smiles, because he saw something she does every day, often invisibly.

Notice the details (her outfit, her effort, her energy)

Description: Don't miss what she's quietly pouring out.

Example: She walks in wearing a new sweater, her hair just slightly different. "You did something new—looks amazing," he says. She grins. *He noticed.*

Praise her to the kids

Description: Let them hear you admire her out loud.

Example: While she's in the kitchen, he tells the kids, "Do you know how lucky we are to have her? She's strong, smart, and kind." She hears it from around the corner—and tears up over the spaghetti pot.

Share a memory you love of her

Description: "I was just thinking about that time you…"

Example: Randomly, he says, "Remember that time you danced in the rain on our trip? That's still one of my favorite memories of you." She laughs, her eyes distant and joyful. "I felt so free that night."

Take a photo of her and compliment her beauty

Description: Capture her when she's not posing—then tell her she's stunning.

Example: She's laughing at a text, curled up on the couch. He snaps a photo without warning. "That's my favorite version of you," he says, showing her. She blushes, "You always catch me at my weirdest." "That's why I love it," he replies.

Tell her she inspires you

Description: Be specific. "The way you handle pressure inspires me to stay steady."

Example: After a long day of watching her juggle chaos with grace, he says, "The way you carry things—without losing your compassion—genuinely inspires me." Her eyes widen, and then soften. That one sentence recharges her.

Say, "I don't know how you do it all, but I'm so grateful"

Description: Affirm the invisible labor. Acknowledge the unseen.

Example: She's folding laundry, scheduling appointments, and cooking dinner. He pauses, hugs her from behind, and whispers, "I have no idea how you do all of this. But I see it—and I'm so thankful."

Mention how proud your younger self would be to have her

Description: Let her see herself through your admiration.

Example: Out of nowhere, he says, "If teenage me saw who I married, he'd probably pass out from excitement." She raises a brow, laughing. "Seriously," he adds. "You're everything I hoped for—and way more."

Thank her for sticking with you through hard seasons

Description: Name the valleys—and honor her loyalty in them.

Example: One night, he holds her hand and says, "Thank you for staying when it got really hard. You didn't have to—but you did. And I'll never forget it." Her silence is reverent—and full of depth.

Tell her one thing she does that makes your life better

Description: Let her see her impact, clearly and directly.

Example: He looks at her and says, "The way you bring calm when I'm anxious—it resets my whole world. Just being around you changes things for the better." She doesn't deflect—she just says, "Thank you."

Surprise & Delight

"Every good gift and every perfect gift is from above…" — James 1:17a (ESV)

Why it matters: Surprise brings delight, which reawakens joy in the relationship. It shows you're still pursuing her.

Why it resonates with women: Routine can wear down romance. When you surprise her, she feels chosen, not just scheduled.

Plan a surprise lunch drop-off

Description: Show up at her workplace with food and a smile.

Example: She's mid-email when her phone buzzes: *"Lunch delivery in 5."* She walks to the lobby and finds him holding her favorite wrap and an iced tea. "Just thought you could use a break," he says. She beams all afternoon.

Gift her a little "just because" token

Description: Doesn't have to be expensive—just thoughtful.

Example: He hands her a small bag at the end of the day. Inside is a keychain engraved with a phrase she once said. "You remembered that?" she whispers. "Of course I did."

Decorate her car with sticky notes of love

Description: Each window filled with a reason you love her.

Example: She opens her car door after work and finds it covered in sticky notes: *"You're brilliant." "You're beautiful." "You're mine."* She calls him immediately, laughing and crying all at once.

Order her favorite food without asking

Description: Sometimes, comfort food speaks louder than words.

Example: She walks in after a long day and smells her favorite takeout already on the table. "How did you know?" she asks. "Because Tuesdays are hard—and *Pad Thai* fixes everything."

Bring home a book she'd love

Description: Know her taste. Let stories be your shared language.

Example: He walks in holding a new book. "Saw this and thought of you—main character's a fierce woman who saves the day." She lights up. "You do know me."

Send flowers to her office

Description: A classic move that never gets old.

Example: She's in a meeting when a bouquet arrives with a card: *"For the woman making moves and making it look easy."* Everyone in the room smiles. She hides her face—but keeps the card.

Set up a "favorites" night (favorite meal, show, dessert)

Description: Make everything about *her* for one evening.

Example: He tells her, "Tonight is all about your favorites." Her favorite meal is ready, her show is queued, her favorite dessert is plated. She jokes, "Is this a trap?" He smiles. "Nope. Just love in disguise."

Hide a small gift somewhere unexpected

Description: In her bag, drawer, or even the fridge.

120

Example: She finds a tiny velvet box in the fridge, right next to the oat milk. Inside? A bracelet engraved with *"Still choosing you."* Her morning goes from routine to radiant.

Buy her a cozy blanket and wrap her in it

Description: Turn comfort into a hug she can carry.

Example: On a cold evening, he drapes a new ultra-soft blanket over her shoulders. "You looked like you needed a hug you could wear," he says. She smiles and wraps herself tighter.

Surprise her by learning something new for her (a recipe, a song)

Description: The effort means more than the skill.

Example: She hears music from the living room—he's trying to play her favorite song on guitar. Badly. But when she walks in, he finishes the chorus. "That was for you," he grins. She claps, tears in her eyes.

Challenging & Growing Together

"And let us not grow weary of doing good, for in due season we will reap, if we do not give up." — Galatians 6:9 (ESV)

Why it matters: Growth doesn't happen by accident. When you lovingly challenge each other toward maturity and better habits, you're sowing seeds for a stronger marriage down the road.

Why it resonates with women: She wants to know you're not coasting through life, but becoming something deeper—together. When you pursue growth side-by-side, she feels like you're building something that lasts beyond feelings or seasons.

Read a marriage book together

Description: Sharpen your connection—page by page.

Example: He suggests they read *The Meaning of Marriage* together. A chapter a week, with tea and honest conversation. It turns into a rhythm they didn't know they needed.

Attend a marriage seminar

Description: Leveling up love, on purpose.

Example: He registers them for a local weekend retreat. She raises an eyebrow at first—but by Saturday night, they're holding hands tighter and finishing each other's prayers.

Take a personality test and compare

Description: Learn each other—quirks, wiring, default settings.

Example: They both take the Enneagram. Turns out, she's a 2. He's a 5. "So *that's* why I always over-explain things," he says. They laugh—and understand each other better than before.

Challenge each other with a weekly goal

Description: Grow on purpose—side by side.

Example: Each Sunday, they pick one goal: this week, no phones at the table. Next week, daily encouragement texts. A tiny challenge becomes a big shift in intimacy.

Journal together once a week

Description: Write memories, prayers, or reflections in the same notebook.

Example: He opens a shared journal and writes: *"Grateful for her patience this week."* She reads it, then adds, *"Still learning grace from the way he listens."* One notebook, two pens, one heart.

Study one biblical couple and reflect

Description: Find your story in theirs.

Example: They read about Priscilla and Aquila, noting how they served and taught together. "I want that," he says. She replies, "We already have it—just on a smaller stage."

Start a memory album

Description: Photos, captions, dates—build your legacy page by page.

Example: He gives her a blank photo book titled *"Our Story (So Far)."* They sit down, print photos, and relive their firsts. Every page becomes a time machine and a love letter.

Learn her love language again

Description: People change. Ask. Observe. Adapt.

Example: He asks her casually, "What makes you feel loved lately?" Her answer is different than before. He listens, files it away, and starts loving her that way—immediately.

Pick a virtue to grow in as a couple

Description: Humility, patience, courage—set a theme, not just a goal.

Example: Over coffee, they decide their word for the month is *gentleness*. It colors their tone, their responses, their choices. And slowly, it rewires how they speak love.

Share something vulnerable

Description: Let her see the soft places. Trust her with your heart.

Example: He looks at her and says, "I've been carrying a fear I haven't said out loud." Then he shares. She listens, without judgment, and simply says, "Thank you for trusting me with that." The room feels safer.

Humor & Lightness

"She laughs at the time to come." — Proverbs 31:25b (ESV)

Why it matters: Laughter brings resilience and intimacy. It reminds you both that love doesn't have to be heavy to be holy.

Why it resonates with women: Laughter makes her feel safe, seen, and light again. Playfulness rekindles connection in surprising ways.

Send her a funny meme

Description: Laughter in her inbox = instant mood boost.

Example: She's in the middle of a hectic workday when her phone buzzes with a meme he found. It's a ridiculously accurate couple joke. She snorts into her coffee and texts back, *"I feel attacked. And loved."*

Tell her your best dad joke

Description: Eye-rolls count as affection.

Example: Over breakfast, he deadpans, "Did you hear about the guy who invented Lifesavers? He made a mint." She groans, "Please stop," while smiling and shaking her head. He calls it a win.

Reenact a cheesy movie scene

Description: Go full drama—bonus points for slow motion.

Example: She's cooking dinner when he bursts into the kitchen and yells, "Don't you *ever* let go, Rose!" then dramatically pretends to sink behind the island. She laughs so hard she nearly drops the spoon.

Play a harmless prank

Description: Laughter with zero damage builds joy.

Example: She opens the fridge and finds googly eyes on all the food. "Did my yogurt just *look* at me?" she calls out. "Your breakfast sees you," he replies from the next room.

Share an embarrassing moment

Description: Humility is disarming. Go first, laugh loud.

Example: He admits, "In middle school, I thought 'déjà vu' was a rapper." She laughs for five minutes and loves him more for not taking himself too seriously.

Make a parody song about your marriage

Description: Rewrite the lyrics to a favorite tune—make it ridiculous.

Example: To the tune of *"My Girl,"* he sings:

"I've got dishes in the sink… and laundry on the floor… but I still got… my girl…"

She throws a pillow at him, laughing so hard she wheezes.

Try karaoke together

Description: Bad singing, great bonding.

Example: They go to a karaoke night and duet *"A Whole New World."* He's flat, she's too loud, but by the last chorus they're holding hands, belting it with zero shame. The whole room claps.

Post a silly couples TikTok

Description: Go viral—or go down trying.

Example: He convinces her to try a dance challenge. Two takes later, they're both doubled over laughing. The video gets 7 views. She doesn't care—she'll remember it forever.

Buy matching socks or PJs

Description: Ridiculous? Yes. Adorable? Also yes.

Example: She opens a gift bag and pulls out matching avocado pajama pants. "You're serious?" she laughs. "Dead serious," he replies—already wearing his pair.

Make a "husband survival kit" with silly things

Description: Duct tape, chocolate, prayer cards—make it hilarious and sweet.

Example: He hands her a shoebox labeled *"Husband Survival Kit."* Inside? A stress ball, a chocolate bar, a tiny Bible, and a note that says, *"For when I forget to load the dishwasher. Again."* She can't stop laughing—and loving him.

Adventures & Memories

"I remember the days of old; I meditate on all that you have done." — Psalm 143:5a (ESV)

Why it matters: Shared memories build emotional depth. Adventure bonds you through joy, spontaneity, and newness.

Why it resonates with women: She treasures meaningful moments. New memories become emotional anchors she'll carry for years.

Go for a spontaneous drive

Description: No destination. Just gas, music, and freedom.

Example: He walks in and says, "Let's drive till we see a sunset." They hit the road, windows down, no plan. Two hours later, they're watching the sky turn gold on a backroad neither of them knew existed.

Take her on a local museum or gallery tour

Description: Culture + curiosity + conversation = connection.

Example: They wander through a quirky art gallery, making up stories about each painting. "That one's obviously about your cooking," he jokes. She elbows him—but can't stop smiling.

Do a couples photo shoot

Description: Dress up or stay casual—just capture the now.

Example: He books a surprise mini session with a local photographer. At first, she feels awkward—but by the third pose, they're laughing like newlyweds. The framed photo becomes her favorite thing on the wall.

Rewatch your wedding video

Description: Cry. Laugh. Remember why you said yes.

Example: One quiet night, he cues up their wedding video. She gasps, "You saved this?" They sit on the couch, reliving vows, dance moves, and awkward speeches—with tears in their eyes and smiles on their lips.

Camp in your living room

Description: Blankets, flashlights, s'mores in the microwave—go full nostalgia.

Example: He builds a blanket fort, lights fake candles, and makes microwave s'mores. "We're glamping," he declares. She climbs in and says, "This is better than a real tent—no bugs, all love."

Create a shared "marriage bucket list"

Description: Dream up experiences—wild and simple—you'll check off together.

Example: He pulls out a notebook and writes "Things We'll Do Before We're Old." They take turns listing items: "Visit Ireland." "Cook through a whole cookbook." "Slow dance on a rooftop." Suddenly, forever feels fun.

Visit the place you got engaged

Description: Return to the beginning. Watch how far you've come.

Example: They drive to the overlook where he proposed. The bench is still there, weathered like them—but solid. "I still remember exactly how you looked," he says. She grins, "Terrified?" "Radiant."

132

Do a sunrise coffee date

Description: Start the day with warmth, caffeine, and togetherness.

Example: They wake up early, grab coffee, and sit on the hood of the car as the sun rises. It's quiet, a little chilly, and completely perfect. She leans into his shoulder and says, "This feels like a reset."

Make a time capsule

Description: Write letters, add keepsakes, and promise to reopen it together.

Example: They fill a shoebox with notes, photos, and a USB of favorite songs. On top, they tape a sign: *"Do not open until 2035."* As they seal it, he whispers, "I can't wait to rediscover this with future us."

Take her to a place she's always wanted to visit

Description: Make the dream trip happen—big or small.

Example: He hands her an envelope. Inside: printed tickets to Charleston—the city she's always wanted to see. "You made this happen?" she asks. "You made it matter," he replies.

Legacy & Long-Term Vision

"The righteous who walks in his integrity—blessed are his children after him!" — Proverbs 20:7 (ESV)

Why it matters: Legacy love thinks beyond today. It builds something your children and grandchildren can stand on.

Why it resonates with women: She wants to know you're building a future together—not just surviving the present. Vision gives her confidence and peace.

Write her a letter to open in 5 years

Description: Speak to her future self with today's love.

Example: He gives her a sealed envelope labeled: *"Open in 5 years."* Inside, he's written hopes, affirmations, and reminders of the love that carries them. She doesn't peek—but her eyes glisten just holding it.

Record a video message for future anniversaries

Description: Capture your voice, your smile, your promises.

Example: He records a short video on his phone: "If you're watching this, it's our tenth anniversary. Just wanted to remind you—you still take my breath away." She watches it the next morning, already crying.

Share a dream you have for your old age together

Description: Let her into your vision of forever.

Example: He leans over during a movie and says, "I picture us sitting on a front porch, wrinkly and still flirting." She laughs, but her hand finds his. "I love that image," she whispers.

Create a vision board

Description: Use pictures, words, prayers—build the future on purpose.

Example: They spend an afternoon with scissors, magazines, and a poster board. It's part prayer, part dream, part doodle. It ends up framed in the hallway as a reminder: *"This is what we're building."*

Talk about the kind of legacy you want to leave

Description: How do you want your kids or community to remember your love?

Example: Late one night, he says, "What do you want people to say about us when we're gone?" She thinks for a moment and replies, "That we were kind. And unshakably faithful." He nods. "Let's live that now."

Read Proverbs 31 aloud with her name in it

Description: Let her hear herself in Scripture.

Example: He reads: *"[Her name] is clothed with strength and dignity; she can laugh at the days to come."* She blushes, laughs, and wipes away a tear all at once. "You mean that?" "Every word."

Pray together for your grandchildren (or future generations)

Description: Even if you don't have them yet—cover their lives in advance.

Example: He takes her hand and prays, "God, bless the generations after us. Let them inherit faith, not fear. Joy, not shame." She squeezes his hand, imagining grandkids they haven't met yet—but already love.

Start a shared devotional notebook

Description: Write reflections, questions, and prayers to each other in one place.

Example: She flips through the journal they've passed back and forth. His last note reads: *"Today's devo reminded me to love you more patiently. I'm working on that."* She writes back that night.

Build a family mission statement

Description: Clarify who you are, what you value, and where you're going.

Example: They sit down and craft a few lines: *"We serve with humility. We forgive quickly. We love out loud. This is who we are."* It's taped on the fridge now—daily vision made visible.

Write a blessing for each year you've been married

Description: Mark your milestones with gratitude and grace.

Example: For their 10th anniversary, he writes 10 blessings—one for each year. Some are funny, some are profound. She reads them slowly, tears mixing with laughter, and says, "This is the best gift you've ever given me."

Filling the Gaps

"Bear one another's burdens, and so fulfill the law of Christ." — Galatians 6:2 (ESV)

Why it matters: Marriage means stepping in when the other is overwhelmed. Filling gaps shows faithfulness in the day-to-day.

Why it resonates with women: She may not ask—but she notices. When you fill in the cracks, you protect her from burnout and show you're a team.

Watch a YouTube video to learn her favorite recipe

Description: Cook it for her—show her she's worth the effort.

Example: He secretly studies a recipe video for her mom's lasagna. The next night, she walks in to the familiar smell and nearly cries. "You made *this?*" "I did," he says, proudly. "And only swore twice."

Give her a day of silence and solitude

Description: No chores, no texts, no pressure. Just space.

Example: He tells her, "Tomorrow is yours—no noise, no demands." She takes a journal and vanishes to her favorite café. When she comes back, she's lighter, clearer, whole.

Build her a bookshelf for her favorite books

Description: A space that says, "I see what you love."

Example: While she's out, he assembles a small bookshelf, fills it with her favorites, and adds a plant on top. When she sees it, she whispers, "You made this… for *my* books?" He nods. "Your words deserve a home."

Surprise her with a mini home spa day

Description: Candle, robe, calming playlist—let the bathroom become a sanctuary.

Example: She walks in to find a fluffy robe, face masks, spa music, and a sign on the door: *"Welcome to Wife Spa."* He even warmed the towels. She disappears for an hour and emerges glowing.

Watch the kids so she can go out with friends

Description: Support her friendships without guilt or fuss.

Example: She hesitates about a girls' night. He says, "Go. I've got dinner and bedtime." She comes home laughing, lighter, and grateful to be loved *with* space.

Be the first to apologize after an argument

Description: Lead with humility. Not pride.

Example: After a tense silence, he walks over and says, "I shouldn't have spoken to you like that. I'm sorry." She exhales—and softens. Conflict turns into connection.

Volunteer to do something she normally does

Description: Step into her world. Take something off her plate.

Example: She starts pulling laundry from the dryer. He says, "I've got it today." She watches him fold shirts— badly—and doesn't correct him. The gesture was perfect.

Start planning your next anniversary now

Description: Don't scramble—invest in celebration early.

Example: Three months before the date, he asks, "Do you want something adventurous or cozy this year?" Her eyes light up. "You're planning already?" "You're worth planning *well.*"

Give her permission to rest—really rest

Description: Say it out loud: "You don't have to earn your rest."

Example: He notices her guilt-tripping herself over a nap. He sits beside her and says, "Rest is holy. You don't have to do more to deserve it." She lays back down—tears in her eyes.

Leave a trail of notes leading to a sweet surprise

Description: Each note = a breadcrumb of love.

Example: She finds the first note on her coffee mug: *"Start here."* Then one in the closet. One in her purse. The last leads to a gift on the bed—her favorite candle, a new book, and a note: *"Just because you're my favorite."*

Faithfulness & Devotion

"Let love and faithfulness never leave you…" — Proverbs 3:3 (NIV)

Why it matters: True love is tested by time and trial. Devotion anchors your relationship in consistency, not convenience.

Why it resonates with women: In a world of fleeting love, she needs to know your heart stays. Faithfulness makes her feel secure and chosen.

Speak vows over her again

Description: Remind her of the promises you still mean.

Example: One quiet night, he takes her hands and says, "I promise to love you through the chaos, the calm, and everything in between." She blinks—caught off guard by the echo of their wedding day—and whispers, "Still yes."

Text "I'd marry you again today"

Description: Because she deserves to hear it—often.

Example: She checks her phone mid-meeting and sees: *"Just thinking of you. I'd marry you again in a heartbeat."* Her face warms, her shoulders drop, and her day instantly shifts.

Thank God for her in your personal prayer time

Description: Even if she never hears it—heaven does.

Example: Alone before bed, he whispers, "God, thank You for her—for her resilience, her love, her laughter. She's my daily miracle." It's quiet, unseen, and eternal.

Write "I choose you" and leave it for her

Description: Post-it note. Text. Journal page. Powerful three words.

Example: She finds a sticky note on her coffee cup: *"I choose you. Still. Always."* It's three words, twelve letters—and her whole heart melts before the first sip.

Do a 7-day fast in part for your marriage

Description: Dedicate a week to spiritual focus and intimacy.

Example: He tells her, "I'm fasting this week—for clarity, strength, and us." She doesn't say much—just places a hand over his heart. She's never felt more spiritually covered.

Take communion together at home

Description: Invite the sacred into the ordinary.

Example: They sit at the table with crackers and juice. He reads from 1 Corinthians and they pray, break bread, and remember grace. The living room becomes holy ground.

Hang a verse about marriage in your bedroom

Description: Let Scripture shape the atmosphere of your intimacy.

Example: Above their bed, she notices a framed verse: *"Two are better than one… A cord of three strands is not easily broken."* He hung it quietly—but it speaks loudly.

Tell her she's your Proverbs 31 woman

Description: Affirm her value through God's Word.

Example: He wraps his arms around her and says, "You work hard. You speak wisdom. You care deeply. You're my Proverbs 31." She laughs—but she also stands a little taller.

Pray for purity and protection over your bond

Description: Guard your covenant with prayer, not just promises.

Example: He prays alone: "Keep my eyes clean, my heart humble, and our love protected." It's not performance—it's preservation. She'll never hear it— but she'll feel it.

Write her name in your Bible

Description: Mark her in the margins of your faith story.

Example: On the inside cover of his Bible, beside *"Prayers & Promises"*, he writes her name. Below it: *"My daily reminder of God's goodness."*

Everyday Love

"Love bears all things, believes all things, hopes all things, endures all things. Love never ends." — 1 Corinthians 13:7–8a (ESV)

Why it matters: The most powerful love is consistent, ordinary, and enduring. Daily love builds the strongest bonds.

Why it resonates with women: She doesn't need fireworks—she needs steady light. When you show up in little ways, every day, she knows she's deeply loved.

Let her choose dinner

Description: Empower her with small choices that matter.

Example: As they both stare blankly at the fridge, he hands her the phone and says, "You pick tonight—no vetoes." She scrolls, lights up at sushi, and says, "Even if I go full spicy tuna?" He smiles. "Especially if you do."

Leave a flower on her pillow

Description: Beauty waiting where she rests.

Example: She walks into the bedroom after brushing her teeth and finds a single lavender stem resting gently on her pillow. No note, no fanfare—just a quiet gesture that says, *I thought of you.*

Refill her favorite candle

Description: It's not about the scent—it's about memory and care.

Example: She lights the last bit of her favorite candle and sighs. Two days later, there's a new one waiting on the counter, same scent, same label. She looks at him. "I noticed it was almost gone," he says. "So I fixed that."

Put a small love token in her Bible

Description: A bookmark, note, photo—anything to say "you matter."

Example: She opens her Bible for quiet time and a small photo of them falls into her lap. On the back: *"Still choosing you—every morning, every night."* Her eyes linger longer on the Word and the man behind the note.

Hold her longer than usual

Description: Linger. Let presence speak where words fall short.

Example: She hugs him in passing, expecting a quick squeeze—but he holds her a few seconds longer. No words, just warmth. When she finally steps back, she smiles. "That was different." "Yeah," he says. "Felt needed."

Watch the stars and talk about life

Description: Slow moments build deep connection.

Example: They sit on a blanket in the backyard, wrapped in a shared hoodie, sipping tea, saying very little. "Isn't it wild that we're small—and still somehow this big to each other?" she says. He nods, watching her more than the stars.

Give her a shoulder to cry on

Description: No solutions. Just safety.

Example: She breaks down mid-conversation, overwhelmed and wordless. He wraps his arms around her without a sound, letting her sob into his chest. No fixing. No rushing. Just being her anchor until she steadies.

Pray for her silently when she's stressed

Description: Lift her in secret when the world feels heavy.

Example: She paces the kitchen, muttering to-do lists under her breath. He doesn't interrupt—just silently prays, *God, give her breath. Give her strength. Give her peace.* A moment later, she sighs deeply, unaware heaven was just asked to help her exhale.

Text her something you loved about today

Description: Let her know what moment mattered most.

Example: In the middle of her afternoon meeting, she sees a message: *"You humming while you made coffee this morning—that's my favorite soundtrack."* She smiles, cheeks warm, mood lifted.

Offer to talk when she looks overwhelmed

Description: Give her space—or invitation. Let her decide.

Example: She's sitting quietly on the couch, eyes far away. He walks over, sits beside her, and says softly, "Wanna talk or just sit together?" She leans her head on his shoulder. "Both," she whispers.

Warm her towel in the dryer

Description: The smallest comforts speak volumes.

Example: She steps out of the shower and he's waiting with a warm towel. "It's not spa day," he says, "but you deserve spa treatment." Her grin is instant—and cozy.

Pick up a book she'd love

Description: Let her imagination know it's worth fueling.

Example: He hands her a wrapped book. "The main character reminded me of you—brave, brilliant, slightly sarcastic." She lights up, already flipping through the pages.

Watch her favorite movie

Description: Yes, even the one with all the crying.

Example: She suggests her comfort film—for the third time. He presses play, arms around her. Halfway through, she's crying, and he's pretending not to tear up. Again.

Tuck a card in her bag

Description: Let her find love when she's not looking.

Example: She reaches for her wallet mid-errand and finds a card: *"You're strong. You're stunning. You're loved."* The world gets quieter for a second.

Offer a spontaneous blessing

Description: Pause. Pray. Speak life aloud.

Example: While folding laundry, he says, "May peace fill your heart today, and may you feel how deeply you're loved." She stops, lets the words soak in, and simply says, "Amen."

Read a chapter of the Bible together

Description: Truth makes every moment richer.

Example: Over breakfast, they take turns reading Proverbs 3 aloud. "That hit different," she says afterward. "So did the way you read it," he replies.

Choose a faith verse for the week

Description: Let Scripture shape your rhythm together.

Example: He writes Isaiah 26:3 on a sticky note and puts it on the mirror: *"You keep him in perfect peace…"* She sees it each morning—and feels steadier.

Walk through a garden and talk

Description: Let beauty soften your pace and conversation.

Example: They stroll through rows of roses and lavender, hands brushing, voices low. "I missed this," she says. "Me too," he replies. Nature heals—and so does time together.

Pray together before leaving the house

Description: Align your hearts before your feet move.

Example: At the door, he grabs her hand: "God, go before her. Give her peace today." She exhales, squeezes his hand, and walks out with more than just her keys.

Praise her character—not just actions

Description: Notice who she *is,* not just what she does.

Example: "You're so steady," he tells her out of the blue. "When things feel crazy, you're an anchor." She looks down, quietly proud to be known that deeply.

Serve her without being noticed

Description: Love loudest in the quiet.

Example: She finds the dishwasher empty, the gas tank full, and her shoes cleaned off—without ever seeing him do it. Just quiet kindness on repeat.

Ask her to teach you something

Description: Let her feel valued in what she knows.

Example: "Can you show me how you make your chai?" he asks. She lights up, explaining spices and timing. The tea turns out perfect—and so does the moment.

Surprise her with her favorite dessert

Description: Sugar + love = magic.

Example: She opens the freezer and gasps: tiramisu. "From that place I love?" He nods. "Had to call three times. Worth it."

Be her loudest cheerleader

Description: Let your voice be louder than her doubts.

Example: As she closes her laptop after a tough presentation, he says, "You crushed that. Seriously— you made it look easy." She believes it—because he believes in her.

Encourage her to rest in God

Description: Point her gently toward peace, not pressure.

Example: She's spiraling with stress. He says softly, "You don't have to carry it all. Let God take some of it." She exhales—and does.

Give her the last bite of dessert

Description: It's not about the brownie—it's about her.

Example: There's one spoonful left. He holds it out. "Yours." She teases, "That's real love." "The deepest kind," he grins.

Turn off the game and talk

Description: Let her be more important than your team.

Example: She sits beside him mid-game. Without hesitation, he clicks "off" and turns toward her. "What's on your mind?" She smiles—game won.

Let go of a small grudge

Description: Choose grace over scorekeeping.

Example: He was annoyed all day. Then he looks at her across the room, sees her tired eyes, and decides, *It's not worth the distance.* He walks over and kisses her forehead.

Bless her family

Description: Love the ones she came from.

Example: He sends her mom a kind message after Sunday dinner. "Thank you for raising someone I admire every day." She reads it later—and hugs him a little tighter that night.

Choose peace over being right

Description: Sometimes love means letting the argument go.

Example: They disagree over directions. He smiles mid-sentence and says, "You know what? Doesn't matter. I'd rather have peace than the point." She raises a brow, then laughs.

Offer to start a joint journal

Description: A shared space for prayer, reflection, or just silly notes.

Example: He gives her a notebook: *"Let's fill this with us—honest, funny, holy."* Page one reads: *"Today, I loved the way you said 'good morning.'"*

Wake her with gentle words

Description: Start her day with kindness, not chaos.

Example: He leans in, whispers, "Good morning, beautiful. I hope today is kind to you." She stirs, smiles, and stretches into the sound of being loved awake.

Send her a sunrise photo

Description: A reminder that light returns, always.

Example: He's up early, takes a quick snap of the golden sky, and texts it with: *"Thought this looked like hope. Thought of you."*

Watch the rain together

Description: Let silence be sacred.

Example: They sit on the porch, mugs in hand, just watching water fall. No words—just warmth, and the holy hush of shared presence.

Slow dance to no music

Description: The moment doesn't need a soundtrack to be romantic.

Example: He pulls her close in the kitchen. "Dance with me." "There's no music." "Exactly." She laughs—but sways with him anyway.

Put your arm around her in public

Description: She's yours. Let the world see it.

Example: At the store, in line, he wraps an arm around her waist. She leans in—confident, seen, and secure.

Show up at her job with lunch

Description: An interruption she'll welcome.

Example: She walks into the break room and finds him there with her favorite wrap and sparkling water. "Surprise lunch date," he says. Her coworkers swoon. She just grins.

Handwrite "I love you because…"

Description: One line. One truth. One heart moved.

Example: She finds a note on the mirror: *"I love you because your kindness makes everyone around you softer."* Her mascara pauses mid-stroke—and she smiles.

Read one of her favorite devotionals

Description: Step into her spiritual rhythm.

Example: She sees him reading *Streams in the Desert*, the one she swears by. "That's mine," she teases. "I want to understand what feeds you," he replies.

Take her out just to talk

Description: No errands. No events. Just the two of you.

Example: He drives them to a quiet café. "No plans, just time." Over lattes, they talk about nothing and everything—and both feel full.

Give her a weekend to recharge

Description: Let her disappear without guilt.

Example: He books her a quiet Airbnb for one. "No kids, no noise, no laundry—just peace." She cries— then packs.

Send her a morning blessing text

Description: Set the tone for her day with truth.

Example: Her phone buzzes at 7:22 a.m.: *"May your mind be clear, your heart light, and your coffee strong. You've got this."* And she does.

Make her feel safe to cry

Description: Don't fix—just hold.

Example: She tears up mid-conversation. "I don't know why I'm crying," she says. He gently replies, "You don't need a reason. I've got you."

Help her with her to-do list

Description: Take one thing off her mind.

Example: He grabs her list, scans it, and says, "I'll handle these three today." She exhales, visibly lighter. "Thank you," she says. "More than you know."

Open her car door

Description: Not old-fashioned—just thoughtful.

Example: As they walk to the car, he opens the door before she can. "Still treating you like the queen you are." She rolls her eyes. But her smile is real.

Clean the bathroom

Description: Yes, even behind the toilet.

Example: She opens the bathroom and it's sparkling. Even the mirror. "Did you…?" He shrugs. "Sanctified the space. You're welcome."

Leave a note in her Bible

Description: Whisper encouragement between the pages of truth.

Example: She opens to Psalms and finds his handwriting: *"You're my favorite example of faith in action."* Her soul smiles.

Listen to a podcast she recommends

Description: Even if it's not your thing—because she is.

Example: He surprises her mid-drive: "You wanted me to hear this episode, right?" Her eyes light up. "Yes!" For 40 minutes, they share a world.

Schedule a couples massage

Description: Rest together. Breathe together. Reconnect.

Example: He books a Saturday afternoon massage. "Just us. No phones. All peace." She melts at the idea before they even go.

Tell her how she reflects Christ

Description: Call out the holy in her.

Example: He looks at her and says, "You make mercy look like muscle. Jesus shines in how you carry people." She tears up—and believes him.

Memorize Scripture with her

Description: Hide truth together.

Example: They write Romans 12:12 on the fridge. A week later, they recite it together—word for word, heart to heart.

Pray for her body and health

Description: Lift up her strength, rest, and healing.

Example: He whispers over her while she sleeps: "Heal her fatigue, strengthen her body, restore her joy." Love becomes intercession.

Bless her dreams

Description: Speak life into her calling.

Example: He places a hand on her shoulder and prays, "Let her dreams flourish, not falter. Let her gifts make room for her." She weeps quietly. Not from fear—but belief.

Let her vent without advice

Description: Your silence can be sacred.

Example: She rants for five full minutes. He listens, nods, and says, "That sounds really hard." She exhales, finally heard.

Read Song of Solomon together

Description: Let Scripture remind you how passionate love is.

Example: They take turns reading chapters aloud— laughing, blushing, and smiling wide. "God really went there," she says. "So can we," he grins.

Surprise her with time off

Description: Clear her schedule without her lifting a finger.

Example: He takes over the calendar. "You have tomorrow off. I'm handling it all." She stares at him like he just parted the Red Sea.

Give her space to create

Description: Honor the artist in her.

Example: He sets up her paints, lights a candle, and says, "I cleared the next two hours—go make beauty." And she does.

Send her a letter in the mail

Description: Old school. Romantic. Worth it.

Example: She checks the mailbox and finds a stamped envelope. Inside: his handwriting, a love note. She reads it twice, heart racing like it's 2002.

Post her photo with a love note

Description: Public admiration goes a long way.

Example: He posts a photo of her laughing, captioned: *"My favorite human. Still can't believe I get to do life with her."* She reads it while sipping coffee—and glows.

Speak words that make her feel adored

Description: Don't just love her. Adore her.

Example: He takes her face in his hands and says, "I still can't believe I get to wake up next to you." She blushes, heart full.

Choose her over convenience

Description: Let sacrifice write your story.

Example: He cancels plans, skips the game, and says, "You matter more." She doesn't ask why—she just hugs tighter.

Lead her spiritually

Description: Be her covering, not her critic.

Example: He says, "Let's pray before we decide anything." She nods, already feeling safer.

Show up with grace, not judgment

Description: Hold her gently when she's hard on herself.

Example: She spirals over a mistake. He says, "We all stumble—but you get back up with so much grace." She wipes her eyes, steadied.

Be proud of her

Description: Let her hear your pride.

Example: He introduces her to someone and says, "This is my wife. She's incredible." She glows—not from pride, but from being deeply known.

Let her go first

Description: In line, in conversation, in consideration.

Example: He gestures her ahead, every time. Not because she's weak—but because she's worth honoring.

Wash her feet

Description: Radical service, humble love.

Example: He brings out warm water and a towel. She stares, emotional. "You don't have to." "Exactly why I will."

Be the man you'd want your daughter to marry

Description: Lead with integrity.

Example: He lives with faith, patience, and gentleness. One day, his daughter says, "I want someone like you." He tears up quietly.

Choose love in weariness

Description: Let commitment carry you when emotion fades.

Example: They're both exhausted. He still whispers, "I love you. I'm with you." She nods—and they keep walking.

Walk in humility

Description: Let repentance and grace shape your leadership.

Example: "I was wrong," he says. "Will you forgive me?" She does—and loves him more for asking.

Model Jesus' gentleness

Description: Power under control. Love without force.

Example: In a heated moment, he lowers his voice, not raises it. She notices—and feels safer than ever.

Commit to unity

Description: We over me.

Example: In every decision, he says, "What's best for *us?*" Not just "me." She never feels alone in the choice.

Protect her heart

Description: Guard her trust like treasure.

Example: He closes the laptop, turns away from temptation, and whispers, "I choose you. Again." She never sees it—but she always feels it.

Cover her in prayer

Description: Let God's presence hold what you can't.

Example: Before bed, he whispers a quiet prayer over her, hand resting on her shoulder. She exhales—and sleeps deeply.

Honor her with your eyes

Description: Let your gaze say, "Only you."

Example: Across the room, he looks at her like she's the only one there. She notices—and still gets butterflies.

Choose her—every single day

Description: Love is daily. Active. Decided.

Example: Every morning, before the chaos, he thinks: *She's still it. Still mine. Still yes.* And every night, he ends the day the same way.

.*Scripture Ready Reference by Theme*

1. Words of Affirmation & Encouragement

Proverbs 16:24 (ESV) "Gracious words are like a honeycomb, sweetness to the soul and health to the body."

2. Acts of Service

Galatians 5:13 (ESV) "Through love serve one another."

3. Romantic Gestures

Proverbs 5:18 (ESV) "Let your fountain be blessed, and rejoice in the wife of your youth."

4. Spiritual Leadership

Ephesians 5:25 (ESV) "Husbands, love your wives, as Christ loved the church and gave himself up for her."

5. Intentional Time

Ephesians 5:15–16 (ESV) "Look carefully then how you walk, not as unwise but as wise, making the best use of the time…"

6. Emotional Connection

Romans 12:15 (ESV) "Rejoice with those who rejoice, weep with those who weep."

7. Personal Attention

Philippians 2:4 (ESV) "Let each of you look not only to his own interests, but also to the interests of others."

8. Support & Partnership

Ecclesiastes 4:9 (ESV) "Two are better than one, because they have a good reward for their toil."

9. Celebrating Her

Proverbs 31:28 (ESV) "Her children rise up and call her blessed; her husband also, and he praises her."

10. Rest & Soul Care

Matthew 11:28 (ESV) "Come to me, all who labor and are heavy laden, and I will give you rest."

11. Thoughtfulness

1 Corinthians 16:14 (ESV) "Let all that you do be done in love."

12. Love Through Touch

Song of Solomon 1:2 (ESV) "Let him kiss me with the kisses of his mouth! For your love is better than wine."

13. Spiritual Growth Together

Proverbs 27:17 (ESV) "Iron sharpens iron, and one man sharpens another."

14. Sharing Her Story

166

Luke 6:45 (ESV) "For out of the abundance of the heart his mouth speaks."

15. Daily Practical Blessings

Hebrews 13:16 (ESV) "Do not neglect to do good and to share what you have, for such sacrifices are pleasing to God."

16. Dates & Togetherness

Mark 10:9 (ESV) "What therefore God has joined together, let not man separate."

17. Creativity & Fun

Proverbs 17:22 (ESV) "A joyful heart is good medicine."

18. Unspoken Gestures

1 John 3:18 (ESV) "Let us not love in word or talk but in deed and in truth."

19. Spiritual Encouragement

1 Thessalonians 5:11 (ESV) "Therefore encourage one another and build one another up…"

20. Protecting Her Heart

Proverbs 4:23 (NIV) "Above all else, guard your heart, for everything you do flows from it."

21. Encouraging Her Dreams

Hebrews 10:24 (ESV) "And let us consider how to stir up one another to love and good works."

22. Everyday Appreciation

1 Thessalonians 5:18 (ESV) "Give thanks in all circumstances…"

23. Surprise & Delight

James 1:17 (ESV) "Every good gift and every perfect gift is from above…"

24. Challenging & Growing Together

Galatians 6:9 (ESV) "And let us not grow weary of doing good, for in due season we will reap, if we do not give up."

25. Humor & Lightness

Proverbs 31:25 (ESV) "She is clothed with strength and dignity, and she laughs at the time to come."

26. Adventures & Memories

Psalm 143:5 (ESV) "I remember the days of old; I meditate on all that you have done…"

27. Legacy & Long-Term Vision

Proverbs 20:7 (ESV) "The righteous who walks in his integrity—blessed are his children after him!"

28. Filling the Gaps

Galatians 6:2 (ESV) "Bear one another's burdens, and so fulfill the law of Christ."

29. Faithfulness & Devotion

Proverbs 3:3 (NIV) "Let love and faithfulness never leave you…"

30. Everyday Love

1 Corinthians 13:7–8a (ESV) "Love bears all things, believes all things, hopes all things, endures all things. Love never ends."

About the Author

Dr. Chuck Carrington, PhD, EdS, MA, is a Christian therapist, educator, author, and speaker with over 30 years of experience working with couples, families, and individuals—including trauma survivors, foster families and children, men recovering from pornography addiction, and the wives healing from betrayal trauma. He specializes in trauma, grief, and loss, with a focused practice in Christian counseling that emphasizes relational restoration in the wake of betrayal, infidelity, and emotional dysfunction.

Dr. Chuck's research explores innovative approaches to loss recovery, process addictions, betrayal trauma, post-traumatic embitterment, and the long-term impact of childhood family dysfunction. Blending biblical wisdom with evidence-based therapeutic models and a down-to-earth relational style, he brings compassion, clarity, and deep insight into how past wounds shape present relationships.

He is the founder of *Connect Christian Family Counseling*, where he walks alongside clients on their journey toward emotional and relational wholeness.

When he's not writing or counseling, Dr. Chuck enjoys reading, researching, leading workshops, and serving in local ministry projects. He also hosts free online support and discipleship groups. This book reflects his passion for bringing a practical, gospel-centered message to those navigating the complex challenges of modern life—helping them rediscover their identity and purpose in God's redemptive plan, and equipping them to grow in truth, strength, and grace.

If You Need Counseling or Help,

Dr Chuck offers Christian Faith-Based Counseling and Coaching in men's recovery from porn and cyber-addiction, Betrayal Trauma recovery for women, and restorative counseling to help heal and recover marriages after betrayal.

For a consultation via telehealth video, contact Dr Chuck to get more information on how to overcome the damage of betrayal and addiction. Use the website below to sign up for recovery and support groups, or to join Dr Chuck's online psychoeducational programs.

If you are looking for marriage enhancement counseling or coaching, Dr Chuck offers online webinars and forums to help Christian couples explore their marriage, and how it conforms to God's plan for marriage, to find forgiveness and healing, or to plan for an extraordinary marriage from the outset for engaged couples.

Believers should ask for the Faith-based community discount for the best possible pricing. Free groups include Healing Hearts for women damaged by betrayal, Overcomer's Group for men struggling with porn addiction and cyber addiction.

CONNECT

www.connectcounselor.com
Connect Christian Family Counseling
757 965-5450

Other Titles by Dr Chuck

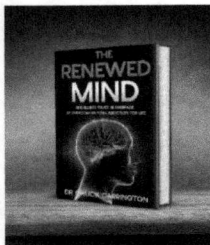

The Renewed Mind: Rebuilding Trust in Marriage by Overcoming Porn Addiction for Life
ISBN# 979-89892386-3-7

Available on Amazon
https://a.co/d/7qwOY7h

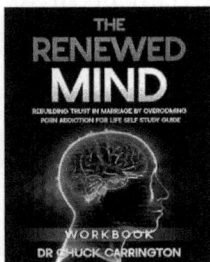

The Renewed Mind companion workbook
ISBN# 979-8-9892386-2-0

Available on Amazon
https://a.co/d/fTPdxoO

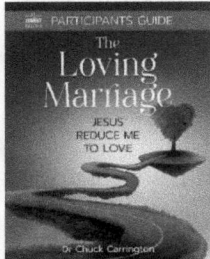

The Loving Marriage: Jesus Reduce Me To Love. Lessons on living out
1 Corinthians in Marriage
ISBN# 979-8989238651

Available on Amazon https://a.co/d/eZttPf8

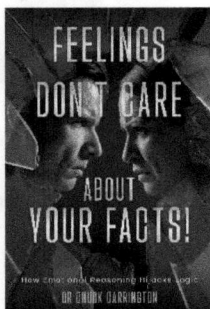

Feelings Don't Care About Your Facts!: How Emotional Reasoning Hijacks Logic
ISBN# 979-8-9892386-7-5

Available on Amazon https://a.co/d/ggF18on

Check out Dr Chuck's *Seven Greatest Hits in Marriage Counseling*, a series of video supported coaching modules presenting his most effective tools to help couples exceed a typical marriage.

www.connectcounselor.com
Connect Christian Family Counseling
757 965-5450
DrChuck@connectcounselor.com
https://connectcounselor.com/group-counseling/

www.ingramcontent.com/pod-product-compliance
Lightning Source LLC
Chambersburg PA
CBHW072011290326
41934CB00007BA/1013